# THE ROMAN HOUSEHOLD

The *domus* (household) was the basic unit of Roman society. This sourcebook illustrates the activities associated with the household, and Roman perceptions of its role and position within the wider social and economic fabric.

A particularly important aspect is the different and frequently conflicting roles and moral values expected from male and female, old and young, free and slave members of the Roman household, and from freedmen and others associated with it. Prominence is also given to legal texts discussing issues which demonstrate Roman concepts of family and household, such as the power of the head of household, rules of inheritance, and relations between patron and freedman.

The 217 newly translated excerpts are taken from a wide range of Latin (and in a few cases Greek) prose and verse literature, ethical and agricultural handbooks and codes, legal texts, inscriptions and other epigraphical material from the second century BC to the sixth century AD. Some of them – including an inscription from Puteoli on the treatment of slaves and the so-called will of 'Dasumius' – are made available for the first time in English.

The fact that other sourcebooks are either more narrowly specific, or heterogeneous and less closely directed at this particular topic, makes *The Roman Household* a book which will be invaluable to students of Roman social history and ancient economic history, and useful to students of comparative sociology/anthropology and the history of the family.

# THE ROMAN HOUSEHOLD

## A Sourcebook

Jane F. Gardner and
Thomas Wiedemann

London and New York

First published 1991
by Routledge
11 New Fetter Lane, London EC4P 4EE

Simultaneously published in the USA and Canada
by Routledge
a division of Routledge, Chapman and Hall, Inc.
29 West 35th Street, New York, NY 10001

Typeset in 10/12 Times by
Mayhew Typesetting, Bristol
Printed and bound in Great Britain by
Clays Ltd, St. Ives plc

*British Library Cataloguing in Publication Data*
Gardner, Jane F.
The Roman household: a sourcebook.
1. Italy. Rome. Social life, ancient
I. Title   II. Wiedemann, Thomas
937.6
ISBN 0–415–04421–9

*Library of Congress Cataloging in Publication Data*
The Roman household: a sourcebook / [edited by] Jane F. Gardner
and Thomas Wiedemann.
p. cm.
Includes bibliographical references (p.) and index.
ISBN 0–415–04421–9. – ISBN 0–415–04422–7 (pbk.)
1. Family – Rome. 2 Households – Rome. 3. Domestic relations
(Roman law) I. Gardner, Jane F. II. Wiedemann, Thomas E.J.
HQ511.R66 1991      90-8691
306.85′0945′632–dc20      CIP

# CONTENTS

# CONTENTS

# CONTENTS

# CONTENTS

# CONTENTS

# CONTENTS

# CONTENTS

# LIST OF ILLUSTRATIONS

# INTRODUCTION

Students and teachers interested in Roman political and social history already have the use of a number of excellent collections of material in translation; one of the earliest was Naphtali Lewis and Meyer Reinhold's *Roman Civilization*, first published in 1951. The emphasis of this sourcebook, the product of teaching on Roman social history at the universities of Reading and Bristol, differs in that it seeks to describe the activities and the often conflicting aspirations of individuals within the household (Latin *domus*), the basic social unit in Roman as in most agrarian societies, rather than the roles and interactions of status groups and economic classes within the wider society. Material on aspects of social history in that wider sense may be found elsewhere, for example, in Jo-Ann Shelton's sourcebook *As the Romans Did* (Oxford, 1988) or Thomas Wiedemann's *Greek and Roman Slavery* (London and Baltimore, 1981).

Social history proceeds by positing 'models' or 'ideal types'; a sourcebook necessarily has to consist, at least in part, of extracts which the editors have selected because they consider them representative or 'typical'. But our intention has been to avoid giving the impression that the Romans had a uniform or self-consistent ideal of the model household. Both practice and ideals changed over time (and it is not always possible to deduce what happened in archaic Rome from later statements as to what it was thought ought to have happened then). There were differences between different geographical regions (we have avoided using the considerable body of Egyptian source material, since much of it illustrates social conditions which differed significantly from those of the 'Roman' household). And even in the same place and period, the differences between the households of the wealthy and those of the poor were not just quantitative, but resulted in different practices and aspirations – for example, in the attitude towards children as a potential labour source; or the wish to bestow property at death by testament rather than according to customary divisions. The moral ideals to which wealthy Roman senators no less than smallholders adhered in public were certainly strongly influenced by what may be called a 'peasant' ideology; but in practice adherence to these values declined markedly as wealth increased. We have tried to illustrate some of the contradictions between ideals and practice; but it is not always easy to evaluate whether particular comments in our sources typify one rather than the other.

If there were inconsistencies and contradictions in the practices and aspirations of the people who are the objects of our study, then they are magnified by the problems involved in interpreting the source material they have left us.[1] Classical literature does not try to preserve 'typical' information for the sake of modern social historians, but often records what is exceptional, amazing and sometimes fantastic. Nor do inscriptions necessarily give us information which is any more objective. As far as the social institution of the household is concerned, few inscriptions – even most of the graffiti scratched on walls at Pompeii – can be taken at face value; they were not intended to be read by those who belonged to the family or household concerned, but were targeted at outsiders. Understandably therefore, inscriptions hardly ever refer to shortcomings, failures to live up to the ideal: they are advertisements of the household's success, aimed at the passer-by. Personal letters are sometimes a better source for evidence about genuine emotions and problems; yet even there, since epistolography was itself a recognised literary art-form in antiquity, feelings may be masked in terms of conventional commonplaces (*topoi*). Every classical literary genre has its own conventions, and the relationship between reality and the behaviour described, for example, in panegyric, a satirical invective, or love poetry, is quite different. Legal texts, too, operate according to their own discrete codes: the world of which the lawyers took cognisance was not completely divorced from actual human behaviour, but nor was it identical. In Rome large areas of activity were regulated by social custom and precedent (*mores* and *exempla*) rather than by the legal rules recorded by the jurists; the *consilium* is a case in point – a major social institution which is almost totally ignored in the legal texts. Nevertheless, legal texts and case-law are a useful source of evidence both for the values publicly subscribed to, and those operating in practice.

Translation involves interpretation. Latin words sometimes contain a range of meanings which were related in the mind of a Latin-speaker, but not in that of an English-speaker. Commonplace moral ideals in particular are notoriously difficult to transfer from one culture to another, and at the same time so important for an appreciation of social bonds, that we have sometimes thought it best to retain Latin phrases alongside our English version. In a few cases we have included the Latin text of an inscription in its entirety.[2]

Numbers in bold type throughout the text refer to the numbered extracts.

Our thanks are due to various colleagues for their help, and specifically to Edward Champlin for elucidating some problems concerning 'Dasumius', and T. G. Parkin (Victoria University, Wellington, New Zealand) for making available to us some of his research material on old age. Ian Jenkins and others helped in the search for illustrations. TW is grateful to Ian Hamnett for the loan of rare legal texts. Richard Stoneman and his team have been helpful as always. The lion's share of the typing was done by TW, for which relief JFG is especially grateful.

JFG/TEJW
Reading/Bristol
Spring 1990

*Notes*

1 There is an excellent short discussion in David Braund's Introduction to his sourcebook *Augustus to Nero* (London, 1985).

2 Square brackets are used to indicate restorations in the original text; editorial comments or elucidations within a text are indicated by parentheses.

# LIST OF ABBREVIATIONS

AE  *Année Epigraphique* (Paris).

CIL  *Corpus Inscriptionum Latinarum*, many vols (Berlin, 1869– ).

FIRA  S. Riccobono *et al.*, *Fontes Iuris Romani Anteiustiniani*, 3 vols (Florence, 1940–3).

Gardner, WIRLAS  J. F. Gardner, *Women in Roman Law and Society* (London, 1986).

ILS  H. Dessau (ed.), *Inscriptiones Latinae Selectae*, 3 vols (Berlin, 1892–1914).

JRS  *Journal of Roman Studies* (1910– ).

Wiedemann, ACRE  T. E. J. Wiedemann, *Adults and Children in the Roman Empire* (London and New Haven, 1989).

Wiedemann, GARS  T. E. J. Wiedemann, *Greek and Roman Slavery* (London and Baltimore, 1981).

ZPE  *Zeitschrift für Papyrologie und Epigraphik* (Cologne).

1. The household of Julius: see p. 1. Reproduced by kind permission of the Musée National du Bardo, Tunis.

# I

# COMPOSITION AND DEFINITION

The photograph opposite is of a late Roman coloured mosaic from Carthage, now in the Bardo Museum in Tunis. The household represented is North African, and dates to the third or fourth century AD; some of its features are peculiar to its place and time – for instance, the semi-fortified character of the actual buildings (centre), and the fact that the master's favourite pastime seems to be hunting (left and right), the popularity of which with wealthy Romans increased as time went on. But the representations of the four seasons in the top and bottom panels are typical of Roman households in all periods. At the top, the *domina* (lady) of the household sits in her garden; the winter season (on the left) is represented by a *colonus* (tenant) bringing her a pair of ducks, two children beating an olive tree to collect the fruit – a scene which can still be seen in the Tunisian winter months today – and a woman bringing the *domina* a basket of olives. On the right, representing summer, a shepherd looks after his flock, while his wife brings the *domina* the rent in the form of a kid. At the bottom left, children bring her fish and flowers, symbolising the springtime; and on the right, the *dominus* (master) himself is seated in his orchard. Behind him a tenant (or perhaps slave) brings a basket of newly-harvested grapes from his vineyard, together with a hare, while another peasant approaches the master with a gift of two live cranes in one hand and a *libellus* (petition) in the other, inscribed *Iu[lio] dom[ino]*, 'To the Lord Julius'. The social power of Julius and his wife over slaves and tenants is based on their responsibilities as the centre of their *domus* as an economic unit, the framework within which most agricultural production takes place.

1

Although largely using the language of Greek political and moral theory, Cicero's treatise *On Duties* (*De Beneficiis*; written for his son's benefit in *c.* 46 BC) expressed the fact that for Romans, as for many Greeks, the household represented the ultimate constituent of the political community. It was the point where the private and the public spheres met. It is not surprising, therefore, that it was also the point where Romans felt some of the greatest tensions between the interests of the community and those of individuals – for example, in conflicts of loyalty between personal relationships (parent/child, master/slave) and the demands of the state, especially in time of revolution or tyranny (Valerius Maximus lists wives and slaves who showed exemplary loyalty during the civil wars: bk 6, chs 7–8).

## 1 Cicero, *On Duties* 1, 53–5

There are several levels of human society. Starting from that which is universal, the next is that of a common race, nation or language (which is what most of all holds men together). Further down comes membership of the same city; for citizens have many things in common – their town square, temples, covered walkways, roads, laws and constitution, law-courts and elections, customs and associations and the dealings and agreements that bind many people to many others. An even closer bond is that between relations: for it sets them apart from that limitless society of the human race into one that is narrow and closely-defined. (54) Since it is a natural feature of all living beings that they have the desire to propagate, the first association is that of marriage itself; the next is that with one's children; then the household unit within which everything is shared; that is the element from which a city is made, so to speak the seed-bed of the state. Next comes the relationship between brothers, between cousins on the father's side and cousins on the mother's side; since these relatives cannot be contained within one household, they leave to found other households, just like colonies. Next come relationships arising from marriage, which bring even more relatives. This extension and spreading of relationships is the basis of communities; for common blood forces men to help and care for one another. (55) It is a great thing to share the monuments of common ancestors, to participate in the same religious rituals, and to use the same tombs.

Although the word 'family' is often loosely used in English to mean 'household', the two must be distinguished. At Rome, as in many other societies based on agricultural production, each household was based on a single stem-family (husband and wife, together with those who depended upon them), to the exclusion of the 'extended family' (brothers and sisters, uncles and aunts, cousins). The dependant members of the household were not necessarily biologically related; they included slaves and children whom the head of the household (*paterfamilias*) had adopted (women could not adopt in Roman law). Another group of family members who might be biologically unrelated were *alumni* ('nurselings'); they might be slave-children who shared the same nurse with the master's free children, or freedmen or foster-children related to the family, or foundlings, and their juridical status might be free or slave. (See E. Rawson, 'Children in the Roman *Familia*', in *The Family in Ancient Rome*, ch. 7; H. S. Nielsen, '*Alumnus*: a Term of Relation denoting Quasi-Adoption', *Classica et Mediaevalia* 38 (1987), 141–88.)

It may be useful to supply a list of relevant Latin terms at this point, with their English equivalents: *pater* ('father', primarily in the biological sense), *paterfamilias* ('father of a family', i.e., the man with authority as head of household), *familia* (normally dependants, especially slaves – but see below), *dominus/-a*, ('master/mistress', expressing the position of an owner *vis-à-vis* his or her slaves), *mater* ('mother'), *filius/-a* ('son/daughter'), *servus/-a* ('male or female slave'), *libertus/-a* ('freedman/-woman', i.e., freed slave), *patronus/-a* (the erstwhile owner of a freed slave).

## 2  *Digest* 50, 16.195 (Ulpian)

(1) Let us see how the term *familia* is to be understood. It has various meanings, for it is applied both to property and to persons. To property: as, for example, in a law of the Twelve Tables[1] in these words: 'Let the nearest agnate[2] have the *familia*.' It has the meaning applying to persons when, e.g., a law says of patron and freedman 'from that *familia*', 'into that *familia*' and here it is understood that the law speaks of particular persons.

(2) The term '*familia*' is also used to mean a certain body of persons, defined either by a strict legal bond between the persons themselves or in a general sense of people joined by a looser relationship of kinship.

(i) In the strict legal sense we call a *familia* a number of

3

THE ROMAN HOUSEHOLD

people who are by birth or by law subjected to the *potestas* (power) of one man, e.g., *paterfamilias* (father of a *familia*), *mater* (mother of a *familia*), son or daughter of a *familia*, and so on in succession, e.g., grandsons, granddaughters, etc. *Paterfamilias* (head of a household) is the title given to the person who holds sway in the house, and he is correctly so called even if he has no children, for we are designating not only him as a person, but his legal right: indeed, we call even a minor *paterfamilias*. When a *paterfamilias* dies, all the persons subject to him begin each to have a separate *familia*; for each individual takes on the title *paterfamilias*. The same will happen when someone is emancipated,[3] for he becomes *sui iuris* (legally independent) and begins to have his own *familia*.

(ii) In the wider sense we use *familia* legally of all agnates: for even though on the death of the *paterfamilias* each one has a separate *familia*, all the same all those who were under the power of one man will correctly be said to belong to the same *familia*, since they issued from the same *gens* (kin group) and the same house.

(3) (iii) We also habitually use *familia* of slaves, e.g., in the praetorian edict[4] under the heading 'on theft', where the praetor talks about the *familia* of tax-farmers. In that passage, not all slaves are meant, but a particular body of slaves got together for that purpose, that is, for tax-collecting. Elsewhere in the edict, however, it is used of all slaves, e.g., in the section 'On armed assemblage and robbery by force', or again in 'Action for recovery': 'should the condition of the goods be impaired by the activity of the buyer or his *familia*'.

(iv) In the interdict[5] 'On violence', the term *familia* includes all the slaves, and sons as well.

(4) (v) Again, *familia* is used of several persons who all descend by blood from a single remembered source (e.g., we speak of the Julian family). A woman, however, is both the beginning and end of her own *familia*.

*Notes*

1 Twelve Tables: the earliest law code, going back to *c*. 450 BC.
2 Under the Roman law on inheritance, the first claim belonged, after a man's children, to the nearest of the agnates, i.e., of those relatives who could trace descent in the male line to the same male ancestor as the deceased. In practice, the nearest agnate would usually be a brother or sister, or brother's child.

4

3 Emancipation was the release of a son or daughter from the father's *potestas*. It consisted of the fictitious 'sale' (*mancipatio*) of the child three times in succession (once for a daughter). Each sale was followed by a manumission; on the first two occasions, the son reverted to the father's *potestas*, but on the third became *sui iuris*.

4 Praetor's edict: to enable the enforcement of existing laws, or provide for eventualities not covered by law, praetors, as the senior judicial magistrates, customarily issued an edict at the start of their year of office, specifying in detail the circumstances in which they would grant or refuse legal remedies. Taken over more or less *en bloc* from year to year, with additions or modifications, these edicts developed into a comprehensive system of rules, which was codified under Hadrian.

5 Interdict: a magisterial command or prohibition in the edict. Application could be made under it for an order to be issued in individual cases.

The peculiarly Roman concept of *potestas* was central in expressing relationships within a household. By giving the head of each household virtually absolute authority over all its members up to his death, *potestas* excluded any possibility that the *pater*'s capacity to manage the household as an economic unit might be challenged, e.g. by an adult son (unless, indeed, it could be proved to the satisfaction of a court that the *pater* had gone mad). *Potestas* in this sense is not a constitutional power; but neither is it extra-legal – it refers to social, not political, relationships.

## 3  Gaius, *Institutes* 1, 48 etc.

(48)  Some persons are *sui iuris* (legally independent), some are *alieni iuris* (subject to another).

(49)  Again, of those subject to another, some are in *potestas* (power), and some are in *manus* (subordination) to a husband. . . .[1]

(52)  Slaves are in the *potestas* of their masters. This *potestas* rests on universal law,[2] for it is observable that among all peoples alike masters have power of life and death over their slaves, and whatever a slave acquires is acquired for his master. . . .

(55)  Also in our *potestas* are any of our children who are the offspring of a lawful marriage.[3] This right is peculiar to Roman citizens, for there are virtually no other peoples who have such power over their children as we have. . . .

5

(97)   Not only are our natural-born (biological) children in our power, as we have said, but so also are those whom we adopt. . . .

(104)   Women cannot adopt by any method, for they do not have *potestas* even over their biological children. . . .

(108)   Now let us consider those persons who are in our *manus*, i.e., subordinate to us as wives. This is also a right peculiar to Roman citizens.

(109)   But whereas it is customary for both males and females to be held under *potestas* (power), only women come into marital subordination. . . .

(115b)   It is the accepted view that if for any reason whatever a wife is in marital subordination to her husband, she acquires the rights of a daughter.

*Notes*

1   *Manus*: originally, at marriage a Roman woman was usually transferred into the *potestas* (called in this instance *manus*) of the *pater* of her husband's *familia*, of which she became a member, leaving her own *familia*. From an early period, however, this transfer began to be avoided, at least in wealthy families, thus retaining the woman, along with rights to her dowry and inheritance, in her *familia* of origin. *Manus* was very rare by the end of the Republic and virtually extinct by Gaius's time (mid to late second century AD). Most wives were either in the *potestas* of their own *pater*, or legally independent, and entitled to own their own property.

2   *Ius gentium*: 'the law of all peoples', i.e., those institutions of private law which the Romans believed every people did or should have, as distinct from those peculiar to one particular community.

3   *Iustum matrimonium*: a marriage was 'lawful', i.e., capable of producing legitimate children, only if the spouses were of legal age, if they or their *patres* consented, and if they had *conubium*, the legal capacity to marry. *Conubium* existed between Roman citizens, but only under certain circumstances between Romans and certain Latins or foreigners. It did not exist with slaves or close relatives. Under the Empire, it was also excluded between the senatorial class and freed slaves, or persons engaged in certain 'immoral' trades such as prostitution or the theatre (see **14**, p. 17).

The distinction between the domestic world and the public, political world of citizens is made particularly clear by the exclusion from the latter of women, children and slaves. By the time of the jurist Ulpian (early third century AD), this rule was no longer being adhered to, as the wording of the following passage shows: 'ought not to' implies that under-age boys of wealthy families were in fact being honoured with civic magistracies, so that a city could draw on the wealth of their family when there was no adult on whom public office could be bestowed – either because the child was an orphan, or because his father was a freedman. This is confirmed by inscriptions from Ostia and elsewhere referring to children who were town councillors (e.g., ILS 6143, 6144). Children even began to be proclaimed as emperors (often jointly with their father) from the time of Septimius Severus on (see Wiedemann, ACRE, ch. 4).

## 4   *Digest* 50, 17.2 (Ulpian)

Women are excluded from all civil and public offices; hence they cannot sit on juries or hold any civic magistracy or bring actions in court or act on someone else's behalf or act as procurators. In the same way children ought not to hold any public office.

The size of Roman households varied enormously. At one extreme was that of the emperor (the *domus Caesaris*), which was unique and included relatives, friends and procurators of the emperor as well as slaves and freedmen performing many minutely differentiated functions, with the result that there are qualitative as well as quantitative differences. Other vast households included that of a freedman called Caecilius Isidorus who died in 8 BC leaving 4,117 slaves, according to Pliny the Elder (*Natural History* 33, 47/135); or the fictitious Trimalchio. Although fiction, the scene draws our attention to the *dominus*'s role as responsible for all the economic activity of the household; to the account books (*rationes*) as the visible symbol of his economic control; to the *genius* as the religious manifestation of his authority; and to his (theoretical) right to punish his dependants.

## 5   Petronius, *Satyricon* 53

A records-clerk (*actuarius*) diverted the desire to dance which had come over Trimalchio by reciting a list which sounded as though it came from the official Roman gazette:
    '26 July. On Trimalchio's estate at Cumae: born: boys thirty, girls forty. Taken from threshing-floor to barn: 500,000 *modii* of wheat. Oxen broken in: 500.
    Same day: slave Mithridates crucified for cursing the Genius of our lord Gaius (i.e., Trimalchio).

Same day: deposited in strong-box because no suitable investment could be found: 10 million sesterces.

Same day: fire in the gardens at Pompeii, broken out at the house of the overseer Nasta.'

'What was that?' – Trimalchio interrupted. – 'When did I buy any gardens at Pompeii?'

'Last year' – said the clerk – 'that was why they have not appeared in the accounts yet.'

Trimalchio grew red with anger and shouted: 'I forbid any estates that have been bought on my behalf to be entered in my accounts if I have not been informed within six months.'

When our ancient sources wrote about the size of a household, it was generally not to refer to economic statistics but in order to make a moral statement. In the Roman world, a public figure would cause unease either by displaying more wealth (in the form of slaves or of his house-building) than his social importance deserved – a sign of ambition – or less – a sign of stinginess or of a too public display of self-control. In consequence, there was a 'safe' number of dependants for a man in public life. When Cato the Younger was a military tribune in 67 BC, his entourage consisted of fifteen slaves, two freedmen and four 'friends' (Plutarch, *Cato the Younger* 9.4); 'fifteen slaves constitute a household' says Apuleius (*Defence* 47); 'I feed twenty stomachs and one dog', says one of Trimalchio's more respectable freedmen (*Satyricon* 57).

It is the large household that is most visible in literary and epigraphical sources. Only occasionally do poets give romantically-coloured descriptions of peasant life, such as Ovid's Philemon and Baucis (*Metamorphoses* 8, 630ff.):

One house only took the gods in. It was small, thatched with straw and marsh reeds; but in it the respectful old woman Baucis and Philemon, her equal in age, had come together when they were young, and in that hut they grew old together, and by admitting their poverty instead of complaining about it they made it tolerable. There is no point in asking about masters and servants there: the entire household consisted of two persons, the same individuals gave orders and obeyed them (*tota domus duo sunt, idem parentque iubentque*).

But households with no slaves at all are rare in literature: even the poor peasant who staves off his hunger by mixing a vegetable mash in the pseudo-Vergilian poem *Moretum* (117ff.) has an aged African woman of servile origin called Scybale to order about. At the family sacrifice of the Terminalia described by Ovid (**37**, p. 38), the wine is poured by unspecified 'others': slaves are not mentioned, but assumed to exist by any Roman writer who was himself served by them.

An architect will assume that the houses he is writing about are those of the wealthy. There are indeed status-differentiations among 'visible' households, but it is taken for granted that the houses Vitruvius's architect builds are for households whose *paterfamilias* plays a role in public life (as described by Cicero, *The Orator* 3, 133). While 'houses' have to be distinguished from 'households', both have a public as well as a private role to play.

## 6 Vitruvius, *On Architecture* 6, 5.1–2

We have discussed the layout of the rooms in terms of the direction of the sun. Now we must look at the criteria for building those sections of a private house which are reserved for the *familia*, and those which are open to guests.

Those rooms which no one is allowed to enter are considered 'private': bedrooms, dining-rooms, bathrooms and so on. But the public rooms are those which people have a right to go into without being invited: entrance halls, courtyards, porticoes and so on. It follows that men of average wealth do not need wonderful entrance-halls, vestibules and courtyards, since their social obligations consist in going to pay their respects to others rather than receiving their own clients.

Those whose wealth comes from agriculture must have room to keep their livestock and produce on display in their entrance-hall; and they need cellars and granaries and storerooms and other rooms inside their houses for keeping produce rather than showing off their wealth. Similarly those who lend money and are engaged in government contracts need houses that are both pleasant and impressive, and safe from thieves. Those engaged in oratory or public speaking need larger and finer houses with room for those who come to hear them. And those of the highest status, who are involved in politics and the struggle for office and have to appear in public, must have high and impressive entrance-halls, wide courtyards and wide porticoes lined with trees to show off visibly how important they are. Furthermore, their libraries and halls should be built as magnificently as public ones, since these men often need to preside over public meetings and cases requiring arbitration or legal judgments in their homes.

The Roman concept of the 'good father', *bonus paterfamilias*, contained within it both moral and economic principles. (See Chapter III, **71** on the *malus paterfamilias*.) It was a widely-held principle that a well-managed household would produce everything it needed; the independence of the free citizen in public life was guaranteed by economic autarchy in private. The view that the good householder will buy nothing, but sell what he can, is found elsewhere – notably in Cato the Elder's advice on agricultural management; he goes so far as to extend to old and sick slaves the idea that everything superfluous should be sold off (Cato, *Agriculture* 2 = Wiedemann, GARS, 203: cf. A. Astin, *Cato the Censor* (Oxford, 1978), appendix 12). For Nepos, who knew Titus Pomponius Atticus (Cicero's friend and correspondent) personally, the requirement that the household be a self-sufficient unit applies even to the education of its slaves.

## 7 Nepos, *Atticus* 13

This man was no less a good householder (*bonus paterfamilias*) than a good citizen. Although he had a lot of money, no one wasted less than he did on buying things or building things. However, he lived as well as anybody, and everything he had was of the best quality. For he lived in the house called 'Tamphilian' on the Quirinal Hill, which had been left to him as his uncle's heir. It was pleasant not so much because of the building, as because of the park. The building itself had been constructed a long time before, and was elegant rather than expensive; he made no alterations to it, except those made necessary by age. His staff (*familia*) was ideal, in terms of utility; but hardly even average, in terms of appearances. It included some highly educated slaves, very good readers and several scribes – so that he did not have a single personal attendant who was not able to carry out either of these duties excellently; and the other craftsmen required to maintain a household were of the same outstanding quality. And he did not keep a single one of these who had not been born and brought up within the household. That is proof not just of self-restraint, but even of frugality. For not having excessive requirements (which can be seen in a number of respects) ought to be thought the mark of a man of self-control; and providing yourself with what you need by thrift rather than by paying for it is a mark of great industry.

Six centuries after Nepos wrote his life of Atticus, much the same continued to be expected of a Roman *paterfamilias*. Not surprisingly, there were few accounts telling the father of a private household how he ought to behave. But the Christian monastic communities of late antiquity were in essence households whose members inevitably shared many of the assumptions of secular society: and the advice which St Benedict gave to 'abbots' (a title derived from the Hebrew word for 'father') would not have caused surprise centuries earlier.

### 8 *Rule of St Benedict*, ch. 2

The abbot must know that any lack of goodness which the *paterfamilias* finds in his flock is accounted the shepherd's fault. But he shall be acquitted if he has exercised all the due watchfulness of a shepherd over a restless and disobedient flock. . . .

He must make no distinction of persons in his monastery. He must not show greater affection for one than for another, unless he finds him better in action or in obedience. Let not the free-born be put before the slave-born, unless there be other reasonable cause for it. If upon due consideration the abbot shall see just cause he may place him in whatever rank he pleases. . . .

He should manifest the stern affection of a teacher and the loving one of a father – that is, he ought to deal with those who are disobedient and rebellious more harshly. . . . The more virtuous and sensible he should admonish verbally on the first or second occasion; but he should chastise the stubborn, the hard-hearted, the proud and the disobedient at the very moment when they begin to give trouble with a beating and with corporal punishment, knowing that it is written *The fool is not corrected with words*. And again, *Strike your son with a rod and you shall deliver his soul from death* (*Prov.* 23.13 and 14).

The *paterfamilias*'s sole responsibility for the economic management of the household was symbolised by his control of the household account books (*tabulae* or *rationes*: 5). These contained information about sales, acquisitions, loans and debts. Without the master's permission, no other member of the household, whatever their age or civil status, could independently enter into a valid financial transaction, since he or she had no property of their own.

### 9 Cicero, *In Defence of Caelius* 17

There are allegations that he is in debt, there is criticism of his spending, there are demands for his account books. See how brief is my reply. Someone in his father's power keeps no accounts. He has never done any borrowing at all (i.e., in his own name). The spending with which he is reproached is of only one sort – the rent for his flat. It was the prosecution that said he was paying 30,000 sesterces. Now I understand why they said it – Publius Clodius's block of flats is up for sale. Caelius rents a small apartment from him at, I believe, 10,000; but you want to please Clodius (sc. by magnifying the value of his property), and have lied to suit his convenience.

In practice, the *paterfamilias*'s power over the members of his *domus* was considerably restricted in the historical period. Nevertheless Romans liked to believe that it was absolute in principle. A Greek commentator ascribed that principle to the mythical lawgiver Romulus.

### 10 Dionysius of Halicarnassus, *Ancient History of Rome* 2, 26

What Romulus enacted regarding reverence and proper behaviour on the part of children, so that they should honour their fathers by doing and saying whatever they might order them to do, is even more honourable and worthy (sc. than his provisions concerning women), and very much superior to our own laws. (2) For those who drew up constitutions for Greek communities set a very short period for sons to be under the control of their fathers, either up to the third year after physical maturity, or as long as they remained unmarried, or until they were entered in the lists of citizens, as I have found in the constitutions of Solon, Pittacus and Charondas. . . . (4) But the founder of the Roman constitution gave the father unrestricted power (Gk *hapasan exousian*) over his sons. That power was to remain until the father's death. He might imprison or beat him, chain him up and send him to work in the country, or even execute him.

One chapter of Valerius Maximus's encyclopaedic collection of *Memorable Doings and Sayings* contains mythical examples of the *ius vitae necisque*, the *paterfamilias*'s purported right to execute those in his *potestas*. But even if historical precedents were claimed for such exercise of paternal authority, they were regarded as peculiar and extreme. Under the Empire, the *pater*'s rights were explicitly restricted (*Digest* 48, 8.2; cf. 48, 9.5).

## 11 Valerius Maximus 5, 8

Examples of fathers' severity against their sons:

The glory of Lucius Brutus is equal to that of Romulus, since the latter founded our city, the former gave it freedom. When his sons were trying to restore the tyranny of Tarquin, whom he had expelled, he was granted supreme (i.e. consular) power and arrested them; he ordered them to be beaten with rods, tied to a stake and executed with the blow of an axe. He put aside the role of father in order to play that of consul; he preferred to lose his heirs than to fail to avenge the community.

(2) When he was tribune of the people, Spurius Cassius was the first to introduce land laws and achieved personal popularity through many other demagogic actions. After he had laid down his office, his father Cassius, following Brutus's example, summoned a council of relatives and friends, condemned him before the household (*domi*) on the charge of having attempted to establish a tyranny, ordered him to be beaten and executed, and dedicated his personal wealth (*peculium*) to Ceres.

(3) Titus Manlius Torquatus was highly regarded for many reasons, and very learned both in civil law and in the sacred laws of the priests. In similar circumstances, he did not even think it necessary to call a council of relatives. When the province of Macedonia sent complaints to the Senate about his son Decimus

Silanus, who had governed it, he asked the senators not to come to any decision about the matter before he himself had examined the case put both by the Macedonians and by his son. With the willing agreement of both the Senate and the complainants, he took his seat at home (*domi*) to investigate the matter, and gave his attention to both sides all by himself for two whole days; and at the end of the third day, having carefully listened to the witnesses, he gave the following judgement: Since it has been proved to my satisfaction that my son Silanus has accepted bribes from allies of Rome, I judge him not to be worthy either of the state or of my own household, and order him to leave my sight forthwith. Shattered by his father's harsh judgement, Silanus could not bear to look upon the light of day any longer, and the following night he hanged himself. So Torquatus had played the role of a severe and conscientious judge; the public interest had been protected; Macedonia had been avenged. The son's shameful death might have deflected his father's sternness. But he took no part in the mourning for his son, and at the very moment of the funeral he made himself available to clients who came to him for legal advice. For he saw that he was seated in the same atrium in which there stood the image of Torquatus Imperiosus,[1] notorious for his severity; and Torquatus the lawyer remembered that the purpose of the custom of placing the images of one's ancestors and their *tituli* (lists of honourable achievements) in the front part of the house was precisely so that their descendants should not only read about their great deeds, but also imitate them.

*Note*
1  Consul 347, 344 and 340, when he defeated the Latin league; he was said to have executed his son for disobeying military orders (Livy 8, 7).

A number of stories are told about how emperors exercised their authority to prevent their 'friends' from applying the ostensibly absolute power of a *paterfamilias* with undue harshness: the most famous concerns Vedius Pollio, whom Augustus is said to have stopped from executing a slave who had broken a valuable goblet by throwing him to some man-eating fish (Cassius Dio 54, 23.1ff.; Seneca, *On Anger* 3, 40.2). The following story was told by Seneca to show Nero how a good emperor should behave; it illustrates how the *pater*'s power was limited not just by some vague force of public opinion, but by the obligation to take the advice of a council of friends and family members.

## 12 Seneca, *On Clemency* 1, 15

I can myself remember how the people stabbed a Roman equestrian called Tricho with their pens in the forum because he had
beaten his son to death. The authority of Augustus Caesar only
just managed to save him from the assault, at the hands of fathers
as much as of sons. (2) But there was no one who did not applaud
Tarius, who found that his son was planning to kill him and
condemned him after looking into his case; he was satisfied with
a punishment of exile, and kept the parricide in a very pleasant
exile at Marseilles, providing him with the same annual allowance
that he had given him before his crime. As a result of his
generosity, no one doubted that the accused had been justly
condemned (even in a city like Rome where wicked men can
always find a defender); his father had found it possible to
condemn him, although he did not find it possible to hate him.
(3) I want to consider this case further: for it involves a good
emperor whom you can compare to a good father. When Tarius
was arranging to examine his son's case, he summoned Caesar
Augustus to his council; the emperor entered the private house
(*penates*), took his seat and took part in the council of another
household. He did not say, 'No: he must come to my house.' If
he had done that, the court would have been Caesar's, not the
father's. (4) After the case had been heard and all the factors
examined, both those with which the young man defended himself
and those which pointed against him, he asked everyone to write
down their verdict, to prevent them from all following Caesar's
opinion. Then, before the votes were opened, he swore that he
would not accept any legacy from Tarius (who was a rich man).
(5) It might be argued that he betrayed a cowardly fear of appear-
ing to want the son condemned in order to increase his own
chances (sc. of inheriting the father's property). I do not agree.
Any private citizen ought to have enough reliance on a clear conscience to ignore critical rumours, but emperors have to respect
public opinion. So he swore that he would not accept any legacy.
(6) So Tarius lost the potential heir next in succession on the same
day as he lost his son, but Caesar rescued his right to give his
opinion freely. Having proved that he had no private interest in

condemnation (something which an emperor must always be careful about) he said that the son should be exiled to a place chosen by his father. (7) He did not impose the ancient penalty of being drowned in a sack full of snakes, nor prison, since he was more concerned about the man to whose council he belonged, than about the man he was condemning. He stated that a father should be satisfied to impose the mildest punishment possible on a young man who had been tempted to commit this crime but had acted half-heartedly (the next best thing to being innocent); he must be removed from Rome and from his father's sight. (16.1) How worthy Augustus was for fathers to invite to their council! How worthy to be selected as co-heir with sons who were innocent! Such clemency graces an emperor; wherever he goes, he should make everything milder.

All children (i.e., boys under 14 and girls under 12) with no *pater* were required to have a guardian (*tutor*); so were all adult women not under the control of a *pater* or a husband (Augustus made an exception for those who had had three children). The function of the *tutor* was essentially economic, to protect property from dissipation, in the interests of the immediate *familia*, and perhaps also of more distant relatives. A *tutor* of a minor was also responsible for administration, that of an adult woman was merely required to give his authorisation for certain transactions. Except for freedwomen and emancipated daughters, this became little more than a formality (see Gardner, WIRLAS, 14–22).

## 13  Ulpian, *Rules* 11, 1 and 27

(1) Tutors are granted over both males and females: for males who have not yet reached the age of puberty, and are therefore vulnerable; and for females both before and after puberty because they are thought to be weaker and ignorant of matters of business and of law. . . .

(27) A woman needs the approval of her tutor if she wishes to go to law; if she accepts a juridical or financial obligation; if she wishes to enter into a civil contract; or if she wishes to alienate property transferable by mancipation.[1]

*Note*

1 Mancipation was a formal procedure of transfer of ownership. The types of property to which it applied were those which formed the basis of an early rural economy – cattle, slaves, land in Italy and buildings thereon, beasts of transport or burden, rural praedial servitudes.

Marriages in which the wife remained in the *potestas* of her father and was not transferred to the *manus* of her husband ('free' marriages) had become the rule by the end of the republic; exceptions included the marriages of *flamines* and of the *rex sacrorum*, where from AD 23 the *manus* was held to apply for sacral purposes only (see Tacitus, *Annals* 4, 16; Gaius, *Institutes* I. 110–15). The validity of a marriage (and the legitimacy of any children) in the classical period did not depend on the proper performance of ritual at a wedding ceremony, but on other factors, such as the intentions of the couple; the existence of *conubium* (their right to enter into a marital relationship); and the permission of those in whose *potestas* they were.

## 14  *Digest* 23, 2.1–6; 8–9; 21–4

(1. Modestinus, *Rules*, book 1:) Marriage is the association of a man and a woman, and the sharing of every aspect of life; a point where human and divine laws meet.

(2. Paul, *On the Edict*, book 35:) A marriage cannot exist without everyone's consent, that is, the consent of those who come together, and also of those in whose *potestas* they are.

(3. Paul, *On Sabinus*, book 1.) Suppose that I have a grandson through one son and a granddaughter through another son, both in my *potestas*; Pomponius writes that they would be able to marry if they had my consent alone, and that is true.

(4. Pomponius, *On Sabinus*, book 1:) If a girl marries when she is under the age of 12, then she will become a legitimate wife when she has completed her twelfth year (and is living) with her husband.

(5. The same, *On Sabinus*, book 5:) A woman can be married to a man who is not present by means of his letters or a (slave) messenger, if she is brought to the messenger's master; but if she is not present, she cannot be married by her husband by means of letters or of her (slave) messenger. For a wife has to be brought

to her husband's house, not to the wife's, as the place where the marriage has its home (*domicilium matrimonii*).

(6. Ulpian, *On the Edict*, book 35:) Consequently Cinna writes: A man who married a wife without being present, and then fell into the Tiber on his way home from a dinner party and died, must be mourned by his wife. . . .

(8. Pomponius, *On Sabinus*, book 5:) A freedman is not able to marry a freedwoman who is his (natural) mother or sister; since the right to marriage has a moral, not a legal, basis.

(9. Ulpian, *On Sabinus*, book 26:) If a grandson wants to marry, but his grandfather (sc. in whose *potestas* the grandson is) has gone mad, then the father's support (*auctoritas*) will be absolutely necessary; but if the father has gone mad, and the grandfather is sane, then the grandfather's consent suffices. (1) Someone whose father has been taken prisoner by the enemy may take a wife if he does not return within three years. . . .

(21. Terentius Clemens, *On the Julian and Papian Law*, book 3:) A son in *potestas* (*filiusfamilias*) cannot be forced to take a wife.

(22. Celsus, *Digest*, book 15:) If a man is forced by his father to take a wife, whom he would not have married if the decision had been his own, then he has nevertheless entered into matrimony, which cannot exist between those who are unwilling; since that appears to have been his preference.

(23. The same, *Digest*, book 10:) It is provided in the Papian Law that all free-born men (excepting senators and their children) should be allowed to have a freedwoman as their wife.

(24. Modestinus, *Rules*, book 1:) It must be assumed that cohabitation with a free woman constitutes a marriage, and not concubinage, unless she is a prostitute.


Latin literature tends to describe social and economic behaviour in moral rather than institutional terms. Julius Caesar's power was extreme, and although no law gave patrons the right to do so, his biographer tells us that he executed more than one of his freedmen. The unparalleled power of the Caesars laid them open to the charge of behaving savagely towards their dependants. But such savagery was taken for granted: as an example of Julius Caesar's clemency, Suetonius (74) tells how, 'When his secretary, the slave Philemon, promised his enemies to kill him by poison, he punished him by nothing more severe than a straightforward execution' (i.e., without preliminary torturing). Caesar's harshness may have been due to his desire to protect the moral reputation of his *domus* (cf. his alleged reason for divorcing his wife: she had to be above suspicion). But Suetonius also implies that buying costly slaves was a moral weakness.

## 15 Suetonius, *Caesar* 47–8

He paid such a high price for reliable and highly-educated slaves that he was himself so ashamed of it that he forbade it from being entered in his accounts (*rationibus inferri*). (48) When he was outside Italy he would normally use two dining-rooms for his dinner-parties, one for those wearing cloaks (i.e., military personnel and Greeks), and one for the Roman citizens, together with the more illustrious guests from the provinces. He was so scrupulous and indeed severe in the administration of his household, in matters both small and great, that he had a baker's legs shackled for serving different bread to himself than to his guests; and he executed a freedman whom he liked very much for having committed adultery with the wife of an equestrian, even though there had been no formal complaint.

## 16 Suetonius, *Augustus* 67

As a patron and master he could be no less severe than friendly and forgiving, and he honoured and made use of some of his freedmen a great deal; these included Licinus and Celadus. When a slave called Cosmus made serious accusations against him, his punishment went no further than shackling. When he went for a walk with his steward Diomedes and a wild boar suddenly attacked them, Diomedes left him in the lurch; but Augustus preferred to accuse him of cowardice than of a crime, and he made fun of an incident that was extremely serious, since the slave had meant no harm. (2) But he also forced one of his favourite freedmen, Polus, to commit suicide when he was discovered to have been seducing married women; he broke the legs of his secretary Thallus for having betrayed the contents of a letter for 500 denarii; and he had the *paedagogi* and servants of his son Gaius[1] thrown into the river with heavy weights tied to their necks because of the insolence and greed with which they had behaved out in the province (Asia) at the time when Gaius was sick and dying.

*Note*

1 20 BC–AD 4; the son of Marcus Agrippa and Augustus's daughter Julia, adopted by Augustus as his son.

It was not only in the household of the Caesars that the master had the right and obligation to adjudicate in disputes involving, and between, slaves. In the following incident, both the dispute and Trimalchio's judgement are staged – which explains why the slaves are allowed to ignore their master.

### 17 Petronius, *Satyricon* 70

Suddenly two slaves came in; they had presumably just been brawling at the water-fountain. At any rate they were still carrying amphorae on their shoulders. Then, when Trimalchio gave judgement between them in their dispute, neither accepted the sentence he uttered, and instead they smashed each other's amphorae with sticks.

Under the Republic, only the vaguest social pressures restricted the master's right to execute his slaves.

### 18 Plutarch, *Cato the Elder* 21.4

Cato continually tried to get his slaves to have quarrels and disputes among themselves, and was suspicious and afraid when they were in agreement. Those who had been accused of a crime which deserved the death-penalty were tried in the presence of his other dependants, and executed if they were found guilty.

Under the principate, imperial constitutions limited the circumstances and degree of punishment a master might inflict.

## 19 *Digest* 18, 1.42 and 48, 8.11.2

(Marcianus:) Owners may not sell their slaves to be made to fight wild beasts, even if they have a criminal character. This was stated in a rescript of the Deified Brothers (Marcus Aurelius and Lucius Verus).

(Modestinus:) Following the *Lex Petronia* and the recommendations of the Senate qualifying that law, the rights of slave-owners who wanted to give their slaves to fight wild beasts were taken away from them. But if the slave has been brought before a court, and the owner's complaint has been found to be justified, then he may be handed over for punishment.

Under the Republic, the power of a master over his slaves extended to the use of torture to uncover an alleged serious crime; later, the emperors legislated to restrict such powers, or to transfer them to officials of the state. But as this account makes clear, even in the Republic the head of a household (in this case, a woman, Sassia) was expected to exercise his or her powers only with the assent of a family council. Sassia was the widow of Oppianicus, exiled during the unrest of the Sullan dictatorship.

## 20 Cicero, *In Defence of Cluentius* 175–8

Exiled and everywhere rejected, Oppianicus was wandering from place to place, and finally went to Lucius Quinctius in the territory of Falerii, where he first fell sick and remained seriously ill for a long time. Sassia was with him, and was treating a certain tenant farmer called Sextus Albius, a strapping fellow, with more familiarity than even the most debauched husband would be able to tolerate while his own fortunes were unscathed. She thought that the chastity required of a legitimate marriage no longer applied now that her husband had been convicted. It is said that a loyal young slave of Oppianicus's called Nicostratus, an exact and truthful source, used to pass a lot of information about them back to his master. In due course Oppianicus began to recover, and could not put up with the Falernian tenant's misbehaviour any more; so he set off for Rome – he used to rent a place to stay outside the city gate – and is said to have fallen off his horse and hurt his side very badly (not being very well); he arrived at Rome with a fever, and died a few days later. The manner of his death, jurymen, is such as to allow no suspicion of foul play; if there was any, it was due to someone inside the walls of his household.

(176) Immediately after his death, that wicked woman Sassia began to hatch a plot against her son; she decided to hold an investigation into her husband's death. She bought a slave called Strato from Aulus Rupilius, who had been Oppianicus's doctor, as though her intention was the same as Habitus's had been when he bought Diogenes.[1] She said that she was going to interrogate this Strato as well as one of her own slaves called Ascla. She demanded that young Oppianicus hand over the slave Nicostratus, who she thought had talked too much and had been too faithful to his master, to be interrogated as well. Since he was a lad at the time, and the interrogation was said to be being held to investigate his father's death, he did not dare to refuse, although he thought that this slave was well-intentioned towards himself as he had been towards his father. Many friends and guests (*amici et hospites*) both of Oppianicus and of the woman herself were summoned; men of rank, respectable in every way. The interrogation was carried out with every form of torture. The slaves' loyalties were tempted with both promises and threats to make them talk when put to the question; but encouraged by the high rank of those summoned to witness the enquiry, I suppose, they stood fast by the truth and said that there was nothing they knew. (177) It was the opinion of the council (*de amicorum sententia*) that day that the interrogation should cease.

Quite some time later, they were summoned again. The interrogation was repeated. No kind of violent torture was spared. Those who had been invited to attend could hardly put up with it; the cruel and unsatisfied woman was furious that her plan was not going as she had hoped. When the interrogator and his instruments of torture were exhausted – although she herself had no wish to bring the proceedings to an end – one of those summoned, a man endowed with every virtue who had held high public office, stated that it was dawning on him that the purpose of the proceedings was not to find the truth, but to force them to say something false. When the others agreed, it was

22

unanimously decided (*ex omnium sententia constitutum est*) that the interrogation had gone far enough. (178) Nicostratus was given back to Oppianicus, she herself went to Larinum with her entourage, regretting that her son would now surely be safe, since not only no true accusation but not even any invented charge could be pinned on him, and not just the open hostility of his enemies, but not even his mother's secret plots had been able to harm him. When she got to Larinum, pretending that she was convinced by the story that her husband had earlier been poisoned by the slave Strato, she nevertheless immediately provided him with a fine and well-stocked shop at Larinum so that he could make a living as a pharmacist.

Cicero goes on to describe (and dismiss) a third examination of the slaves, three years later.

*Note*

1  Habitus had bought Diogenes, a physician's slave who had been bribed to poison him, in order to make the plot public by obtaining evidence from him under torture (paragraph 47).


We cannot assess how routine the torture and execution of slaves was. The ideal that slaves were loyal (*fideles*) to the master who ensured their social and often physical existence conflicted with another element, the constant fear that a citizen's slaves might turn against him, as expressed by Livy (3, 16.3: 'everyone has an enemy within his own household', *suus cuique domi hostis*), and Seneca (*Letter* 47.5: 'every slave is an enemy', *tot hostes quot servi*). Some historians believe that slaves needed to be systematically terrorised into obedience, for example by the extremely public execution of slave criminals in the arena. Nevertheless public opinion imposed limits to the savagery of masters such as Vedius Pollio (see p. 14 above). As in other societies, such control on the legally absolute powers of owners was expressed in terms of divine protection.


## 21  Valerius Maximus 1, 7.4

The following dream also pertains to the religion of the state. At the Plebeian Games, a certain *paterfamilias* had his slave brutally flogged and led him to execution, bearing the 'fork' (i.e., the cross-beam used for crucifixion), through the Circus Flaminius just before the sacred procession entered. Jupiter commanded Titus Latinius, an ordinary citizen, in a dream to tell the consuls that he had not been pleased with the warm-up act at the last Circus Games. Unless they expiated this by repeating the Games, no small danger to the state would ensue.

Under the principate, the state restricted the rights of masters to act without a court judgment (19 above, p. 21). This did not of course mean that slaves did not continue to be executed; but now that could only be done with the approval of a public court, rather than of the more amenable family council.

An inscription from the colony of Puteoli lays down regulations for the conduct of funerals, which in the Roman world were normally contracted out to firms of professional undertakers. The same firms also contracted for the punishment and execution of slaves, whether after condemnation by a public court or at the request of their masters. For completeness, the entire text is given here, in so far as it can be reconstructed. Column I is fragmentary. It apparently specified those services which, in certain circumstances, the contractors were obliged to provide free of charge for the disposal of dead bodies. It also gave a detailed tariff for specific funerary services. The text of the final section is continuous with column II.

## 22  AE 1971, no. 88 (Puteoli)

Then to the contractor (col. II, line 1) or to his partner, as often as anyone shall throw out [a corpse unburied(?)],[1] he shall pay a fine of 60 sesterces per body, and the magistrate shall enforce judgment for recovery of this sum in accordance with the law of the colony.

The workforce which shall be provided for this undertaking is not to live on this side of the tower[2] where the grove of Libitina[3] stands today. They are to take their bath after the first hour of the night. They are to enter the town only for the purpose of collecting or disposing of corpses, or inflicting punishment, and on condition that whenever any of them enters or is in the town, then he is to wear on his head a distinctive (*coloratum*) cap. None of them is to be over 50 years of age or under 20, nor have any sores, nor be one-eyed, maimed, lame, blind or branded. The contractor is to have no fewer than thirty-two operatives.

If anyone wishes to have a slave – male or female – punished privately, he who wishes to have the punishment inflicted shall do so as follows. If he wants to put the slave on the cross or fork, the contractor must supply the posts, chains, ropes for floggers and the floggers themselves. The person having the punishment inflicted is to pay 4 sesterces for each of the operatives who carry the fork, and the same for the floggers and for the executioner.

The magistrate shall give orders for such punishments[4] as he exacts in his public capacity, and when orders are given (the contractor) is to be ready to exact the punishment. He is to set up crosses and supply without charge nails, pitch, wax, tapers and anything else that is necessary for this in order to deal with the condemned man. Again, if he is ordered to drag away the corpse with a hook, the work-gang is to be dressed in red and ring a bell[5] while dragging away the body, or bodies if there are several.[6]

Anyone who wishes any of the services listed in this regulation to be provided is to notify, or have notification made to the public contractor or to his associate or to the person responsible for the matter concerned, or, if he shall not be present, to such premises as he shall have hired or established for the conduct of the work of funeral director, as to the day, place and nature of the service he wishes to have performed. Once notification is made, then the contractor or his associate or the person responsible shall carry out the commission for the person giving notice first, and then for the rest in order of receipt of notice, unless notice is received for the funeral of a decurion, or for a mass[7] funeral. These are to be given precedence. The order of the rest of the funerals, however, must be adhered to, and they are to send those things whose supply is required by this regulation and supply what is to be supplied.

If a commission is given [to remove] a hanged man, he (the contractor) is to see to its fulfilment and the removal (of the body) within the hour. If it is for a male or female slave, if the notification is received before the tenth hour, removal is to be effected the same day; if after the tenth hour, then before the second hour on the following day.

If the contractor or his associate or the person responsible delays in sending workmen or anything else required by this regulation, then the person holding the funeral or in charge of the matter may without prejudice hire what is required. Whatever he hires or rents or makes use of for this purpose he is not bound to supply or provide, and the same applies to someone acting in a public capacity. Whatever the additional cost of hire or rent, the contractor, or his associate, or the person responsible is to reimburse twice the cost of such hire or rent, as a penalty, and the magistrate shall enforce judgment for recovery of this sum in accordance with the law of the colony.

(The remainder of column II is fragmentary. It apparently provides for fines in the event of default on public orders, with a pledge for their payment. Most of column III is also fragmentary, and appears to deal with such matters as the performance of these services by unauthorised persons; settlement of disputes over faulty performance of contract; numbers of associates permitted; details of materials to be supplied free.)

## Column III (conclusion)

The contractor is to display a copy of this regulation on such premises as he shall have hired or established for the conduct of the work of funeral director, in such a way that it may be read clearly.

If the contractor, or his associate, or the person responsible does anything contrary to this regulation, or fails to do any of those things prescribed under this heading, then for each separate item he is to [pay] into the treasury of the colony [a fine] of 100 sesterces, and the magistrates are to take and exact a pledge for payment of these fines.

*Notes*

1 Perhaps the way some people tried to dispose cheaply of dead slaves; and possibly also done by the 'underclass' of paupers.
2 *Intra turrem* (?). L. Bove (*Labeo* 1967) translates 'take up residence in'.
3 A Latin deity of death and burial. In Rome, and perhaps elsewhere, deaths were registered in her temple, which was outside the city boundary. The restrictions on the funeral gang's freedom of movement within the city were presumably connected with the religious pollution involved in their activities.
4 *Supplicia* can also mean torture; slaves giving evidence sometimes had to do so under torture.
5 For the use of the bell, see Plautus, *Truculentus* 781–2.
6 Various translations are possible; the Latin reads *opera russata id cadaver ubi plura cadavera erunt cum tintinnabulo extrahere debebit*.
7 The text reads *funus acervum*; L. Bove (*Labeo* 1967) interprets as = *acerbum*, 'a premature death', though it is not clear why such a funeral should be given precedence.

One of the most inhumane provisions of Roman law was the extension of guilt for the killing of a master to all the slaves who were under the same roof at the time, whether or not they could have carried out their obligation to come to his help (the *Senatusconsultum Silanianum* of AD 10).

### 23 *Digest* 29, 5 (Ulpian)

(1) Since no household would be safe if slaves were not forced by the threat of danger to their own lives to protect their masters against enemies both from within and from outside the household; therefore Senatorial Recommendations were passed providing for the interrogation by the state of the slaves of persons who have been murdered. . . .

(17) The jurist Labeo says that the term 'those murdered' includes anyone who has died as the result of violence or bloodshed, including anyone who has been throttled, strangled, thrown over a cliff, struck with a stick or missile, or killed by means of some other weapon. (18) But if anyone has been done away with by poison or some other method of killing a person secretly, then his death will not be avenged under the terms of this Senatorial Recommendation. The reason is that slaves must be punished for every occasion on which they failed to assist their master when they could have given him assistance in the face of a violent attack, but did not do so; but what could slaves do to protect him from those intending to harm him by poison or in some other way? . . .

(22) Silanus's *Senatusconsultum* does not apply when someone has committed suicide. Nevertheless his death will be avenged according to the rule that if he killed himself in the presence of his slaves, and they might have been able to stop him, then they are to suffer punishment; but if they were not able to do so, then they are to be acquitted. . . .

(27) Let us consider how the phrase 'under the same roof' is to be understood. Does it mean within the same walls, or within the same dwelling, or the same room, the same household, the same gardens, or the same estate? Sextus says that courts have frequently adjudicated that all those should be punished as being 'under the same roof' who were somewhere where they would have been able to hear the master's voice (sc. shouting for help),

though of course some people have a louder voice than others, and not everyone can hear equally well. (28) The Deified Emperor Hadrian seems to have ruled similarly in the following rescript:

On occasions when slaves are able to come to the help of their masters, they ought not to have more regard for their own safety than for that of their masters. The slave girl who was sleeping in the same bedroom as her mistress could certainly have been able to do something to help her, if not physically then at least by shouting out so that someone in the house or nearby might hear her; that is proved by the very fact that she said that the murderers had threatened to kill her if she cried out. She therefore deserves to suffer the penalty of death, so that no other slaves should think that, when their masters are in danger, they should look out for their own interests.

(29) This rescript has several implications. There is no mercy for a slave who was in the same room. There is no mercy for someone who was afraid of being killed herself. Slaves have to assist their masters, even if just by shouting out.

The family council exerted a shadowy, but real, control over the *dominus*, even though it had no legal standing. One procedure which was carried out in the presence of the family council was the 'informal' manumission of slaves. Again, evidence from the sixth century AD may be the best guide to how the council worked in earlier periods.

## 24 *Rule of St Benedict,* ch. 3

Summoning the brothers to a council.

Whenever any matters of great importance have to be transacted in the monastery, the abbot should call together the entire community, and himself state what it is that has to be discussed. After hearing the advice of the brethren, he should consider it in his own mind, and then do what he shall judge most expedient. We have said that all must be invited to the council, because the Lord often reveals what is best to a younger member. The brethren should give their advice with all humble subjection, and not be forward in defending their own opinion. The decision should be left to the abbot, so that everyone accepts whatever it

COMPOSITION AND DEFINITION

is that he decides is beneficial. Just as pupils should obey the teacher, so it is his responsibility to make all arrangements with forethought and justice. . . .

If anything of less importance has to be done in the monastery, let the abbot take advice of the seniors only, as it is written, '*Do everything with counsel, then you shall not repent of it afterwards*' (*Eccl.* 32: 24).

# II

# THE HOUSEHOLD AS FOCUS
# OF EMOTION

The ideal of living in a self-sufficient rural *domus* affected writers for whom it can hardly have been a reality. In the following fantasy which the poet Tibullus claims he had when his beloved Delia lay sick, he visualises the lady of the household serving a rich visitor herself: a theme which romanticises the drudgery of rural poverty – since in all but the poorest homes, there would be slaves to perform such functions.

## 25  Tibullus 1, 5.19–35

In my madness, I imagined what a happy life I would have, if you were to recover. The god refused it. I would live in the country, and Delia would look after the grain. The threshing-floor would winnow the harvest in the hot sun; she would attend to the grapes in the full tubs, and the sparkling must would be trodden with quick-moving feet. She would grow used to counting the cattle; the chattering slave-child (*verna*) would learn to play in its doting mistress's lap. She would know how to sacrifice to the farmer's god – grapes for the vines, ears of grain for the corn-crop, a libation for the flock. She would manage them all, everything would be under her care; and I would be happy to have no say in the house. My friend Messalla[1] would come to visit; Delia would pluck choice apples for him from our best trees. And when she had greeted the man as befits his greatness, she would look after him carefully, prepare a meal for him, and serve it to him herself. This was my fantasy.

*Note*

1  The poet's real-life patron Marcus Valerius Messalla Corvinus (64 BC–AD 8).

Religious rituals symbolise the real social power of institutions. The divine powers that hold a household together include the Genius of the master, and the Juno of his wife; the Penates, representing the power which the storeroom has to ensure survival; the Vesta, representing the power of the hearth; the Lares, who watch over the dividing line between one household and another; and many other spirits whose co-operation ensured success in household activities.

Although a satirical novel, Petronius's *Satyricon* with its account of a banquet given by the rich freedman Trimalchio shows, in travesty, some of the religious observances of a Roman household.

## 26  Petronius, *Satyricon* 60

A dish with a number of cakes on it had been placed on the dinner-table. In the middle there was a Priapus baked by a confectioner, holding up every kind of fruit and grapes from his enormous groin in the normal fashion. We avidly stretched out our hands to the display, and suddenly a new trick renewed our interrupted laughter. For each of the cakes and fruits began to ooze with saffron if it was touched ever so slightly, and the horrible liquid squirted right on to our faces. So we thought that if the dish had such magic accoutrements, it must be sacred, and got up to pray 'Good fortune to the Augustus, Father of the Community (*pater patriae*).' But even after this prayer there were some who grabbed the fruit, and we filled up our napkins with it, especially myself, since I thought that I could never have a sufficiently large gift to place in my boyfriend Giton's lap.

As this was going on, three boys entered with their white tunics ritually tucked into their belts. Two of them placed images of the Lares wearing *bullae*[1] round their necks on the table, the other carried a dish of wine round and cried, 'May the gods be favourable.'[2] He said that one of them was called Gain, one Good Fortune, and the third Profit. We were embarrassed not to pay our respects to the likeness of Trimalchio (i.e., his Genius), since everyone else was kissing it.

*Notes*

1  *Bulla*: an amulet given at birth to Roman children of citizen status; when boys came of age (see **132**, p. 111), or girls married, the *bulla* would be dedicated to the household Lares. Trimalchio's Lares are being made to suggest the fiction that their owner was free-born.

2  Servius's commentary on Virgil, *Aeneid* 1,730, tells us that after the removal

of the main course, there was customarily a solemn silence, while some food was burned as an offering and a boy proclaimed *dii propitii*, 'May the gods be favourable.'

Dedications to the Genius are occasionally found on inscriptions, although these were generally aimed at outsiders who would have no personal interest in the Genius of an unrelated household (worshipping the Genius of the imperial household symbolised that that household exercised patronage over all Romans: see Cassius Dio 51, 19.7 and Horace, *Odes* 4, 5.31ff.).

### 27   ILS 3025  =  CIL III, 6456 (Aquincum/Budapest)

To Jupiter Best and Greatest who Saves:
and to the Genius of his household, Lucius Serenius Bassus, centurion of the Second Legion *Adiutrix*, for having been freed from a most serious illness; he willingly and properly fulfilled his vow.

While supreme life-sustaining power was ascribed to the head of the household, there was also a divine power which enabled his wife to play her role in creating and sustaining life, the 'Juno'; each household, just as each city of Italy, had such a Juno, though few of them are referred to in inscriptions. This one is from North Africa.

### 28   ILS 3644  =  CIL VIII, 3695 (Lambaesis, North Africa)

To the most mild and loving Genius of her husband Lucius Spellatus Saturninus, and to her own Juno, Horatia daughter of Quintus had this made.

A small number of inscriptions similarly honour the Penates. This one came from York, and is now in the Ashmolean Museum, Oxford.

# THE HOUSEHOLD AS FOCUS OF EMOTION

**29   ILS 3598 = CIL VII, 237 = RIB 649 (York)**

To Jupiter Best and Greatest,
and to the gods and goddesses of hospitality, and to the
Penates, for preserving his own well-being and that of his
(family): Publius Aelius Marcianus, cohort prefect, dedicated
this altar in fulfilment of a vow (?).

All the dependants of the master of a household owed their existence
to his Genius, i.e., power to generate or sustain life. This applied to
adoptive children as much as to biological children, and to slaves as
much as to blood-relatives.

**30   ILS 3643 = CIL VI, 259 (Rome)**

Genio
Similis
familia

To the Genius of Similis, the slaves.

**31   ILS 3604 = CIL II, 1980 (Adra, South Spain)**

The freedman Suavis and the overseer Faustus, the foremost
among the dependants (*prim. in familia*), presented and gave the
Lares and Genius together with the shrine out of their own
money.

The Lares were the gods who looked after movement across the boundaries of a household (hence there were also Lares to be propitiated for
crossing the sea, and crossroads were a particularly important place
where they needed to be placated). Here a freedman thanks the Lares of
his hut or house for having heard his prayer for the safe return of his
mistress; we may assume that great misfortune would have come upon
Eutychus if she had failed to come to his aid in time.

## 32  ILS 3608 = CIL IX, 723 (Morrone, near Lerins, South France)

Gaius Salvius Eutychus, to the Lares who look after his hut (*Lar.cas.*), in fulfilment of a vow for the return of his mistress Rectina.

As polytheists, the Romans ascribed a separate identity to the divine power manifesting itself in each category of experience. Apart from the great gods worshipped by the state, the experiences of daily life too had their divinities. The multiplicity of such gods was greeted with incomprehension by monotheists in late antiquity. Some pagan theorists argued that these deities were simply different aspects of the one ultimate godhead; in an attempt to pour scorn on such attempts to 'save' traditional religion, St Augustine lists many of the gods and goddesses of ordinary life.

## 33  Augustine, *The City of God* 4, 11

Should we also suppose that this ultimate godhead is visible in that multitude of so-called plebeian gods? Let him be in charge of men's seed in the person of *Liber*, and of that of women as *Libera*; let him be *Diespater*, to bring children into the light of day; *Mena*, whom the Romans put in charge of women's monthly periods; *Lucina*, who is called on for help in childbirth. Let him be called *Ops* for helping the new-born by placing them on the surface of the earth; when he opens the infant's mouth for the first time to let him cry, let him be called *Vaticanus*; as *Levana*, let him look after the raising-up of the new-born child from the ground; as *Cunina* let him be said to guard the child's cradle. They say that one aspect of Jupiter is as the three fates, the *Carmentes*, who decide the new-born child's future; as *Fortuna*, let him be invoked as the god of chance. The breast was called 'ruma' in archaic times: as *Rumina*, let him be the god of breast-feeding. When supervising children's drinking, they call him *Potina*, when supervising their eating, *Educa*. When children are scared, he overcomes them as *Paventia*. When hope comes, let him be *Venilia*; when pleasure, *Volupia*; when there is activity, *Agenoria*, and when men are goaded to excessive activity, *Stimula*; when they work hard, *Strenia*. When they learn to count,

call him *Numeria*; when they learn to sing, *Camena*. Let him be
the god *Consus* who offers good advice, and *Sentia*, goddess of
experience; let him appear as the goddess *Juventas* when a young
man lays aside his child's toga, and as *Fortuna Barbata* when he
first grows a beard. The heathen do not even bother to do their
young men the honour of giving this divinity a masculine name;
he might be *Barbatus* (from 'barba', as *Nodutus* from 'nodus'),
or be called *Fortunius* as a bearded god – but certainly not
*Fortuna*. Let him be the god *Jugatinus* when joining man and wife
in marriage; at the moment when the bride's girdle is removed, let
him be called upon as *Virginensis*. Let him appear as *Mutunus* or
*Tutunus*, the phallic god whom the Greeks call *Priapus*. If it
causes no embarrassment, let Jupiter appear in all these aspects,
and many that I have not listed here.

Since all major undertakings required the correct performance of
religious actions, instructions about maintaining the support of the gods
had to be included in agricultural textbooks. We may note that in the
ancient ceremony of purification described by the Elder Cato, Mars had
not yet become a god of warfare, but was still primarily conceived of as
a protector of the fields.

### 34 Cato, *Agriculture* 138–41

(138) On feast days, oxen may be yoked. The following jobs
may be done: they may pull wood, beanstalks and grain that has
to be stored. The only feast days that apply to horses, mules and
donkeys are those of the household (*in familia*).

(139) Cutting down a copse of trees in the Roman fashion has
to be done as follows. Sacrifice a pig, and pray as follows:
'Whatever god or goddess you are to whom this is sacred, you
have the right to the sacrifice of a pig in return for the cutting of
this sacred copse; may it be right to do it, whether I do it or
anyone acting on my orders; therefore by sacrificing this pig in
expiation I make this prayer, that you may be willing to be
propitious towards me, my household, my servants (*familia*) and
my children; for this purpose I sacrifice this pig to you in expiation.'

(140) If you wish to dig up the ground, make another

expiatory offering in the same way, adding the following words: 'In order to undertake this work.' While the work is going on, make the sacrifice in a different place every day. If the work stops for a time or a public or family feast-day intervenes, then make a new expiatory sacrifice.

(141)  This is the way to purify a field. Order the *suovetaurilia* [procession of a pig, a sheep or lamb and a bull or calf] to be led round. 'With the gods' approval, and for a successful outcome, I order you, Manius, to bring and drive this *suovetaurilia* around whatever part of my farm, field and land you think necessary in order to purify it.' First offer some wine to Janus and Jupiter, and pray: 'Father Mars, I pray and beseech you that you be well-wishing and propitious to me and my household and our servants, for which reason I have ordered a *suovetaurilia* to be led around my field, land and farm, in order that you should defend, prevent, and turn away plagues whether seen or unseen, barrenness and devastation, destruction and bad weather; and to allow the fruits, grain, vines and plants to grow and ripen; that you may keep my shepherds and my flocks safe and grant me, my household and my servants strength and good health; for this reason, and in order to purify my farm, land and field, as I have said, accept the sacrifice of this *suovetaurilia*.' Make a pile of offering-cakes with a knife, then present the sacrifice. When you sacrifice the pig, the lamb and the calf, you must pray: 'For this reason accept the sacrifice of the *suovetaurilia*.' It is not permitted to mention the pig, lamb and calf by name. If all victims reveal bad omens, then pray as follows: 'Father Mars, since there is something unacceptable to you in these young victims of the *suovetaurilia*, I expiate them with another *suovetaurilia*.' But if one or two reveal doubtful omens, then pray as follows: 'Father Mars, since there is something unacceptable to you in this pig, I expiate it with another pig.'

Some literary accounts also give expression to a landowner's obligations to look after the religious affairs of his estates.

## 35  Pliny, *Letters* 9, 39

Gaius Plinius greets his friend Mustius.

The soothsayers advise me that I ought to rebuild a temple of Ceres which stands on my estate, to make it better and bigger. It is certainly old and cramped, considering how crowded it gets on a feast day. (2)  A great mass of people from the whole region gathers there on 13 September, there is a lot of activity, many solemn vows are made and many are discharged – but there is nowhere nearby for people to take refuge either from the rain or from the sun. (3)  So I believe that I will be acting out of both civic and religious duty (*munifice simul religioseque*) if I have as beautiful a shrine as possible constructed, and I will add colonnades to the shrine; the former for the goddess's use, the latter for men's. (Pliny continues with instructions for the architect.)

We may note the involvement in religious ritual both of an absentee landowner's guest *amicus*, and of his manager (*vilicus*). Like **25**, this is an example of poetic idealisation.

## 36  Martial, *Epigrams* 10, 92

Marrus, my life-long companion, you who prefer a life of retirement and whom ancient Atina is proud to have as a citizen, I commend to you this pair of pine-trees, glory of this rural grove, and the Fauns' holm-oaks, and these altars of the Thunderer and of unkempt Silvanus which my overseer (*vilicus*) built with his own half-taught hands, and which he frequently stained with the blood of lamb or kid; and our Lady the Virgin goddess of this holy temple, and the Mars you see there as the guest of his chaste sister, Mars who brings me my birthday; and the laurel grove of beloved Flora, into which she fled from Priapus's pursuit. Whenever you placate all this divinity of the little farm with a blood-sacrifice or with incense, please pray that 'wherever your Martial is, although absent he is here as a priest at my right hand, praying to you; imagine him to be present, and grant to both of us whatever each of us prays for.'

The boundary (*terminus*) where two estates and their conflicting interests met was a dangerous place, and the divine power located there needed to be placated annually by the two households concerned.

### 37  Ovid, *Fasti* 2, 639–56

23 February: the Terminalia.

When the night has ended, let the god who serves as a marker to divide up the plough-land be honoured with the customary respect. Terminus, whether you are a stone or a wooden stump buried in the field, your power also has been respected since antiquity. Two landowners crown you from different sides, they bring you two garlands and two sacrificial cakes. There is an altar to which the peasant woman herself brings fire taken from the warm hearth in a piece of pottery. An old man chops up firewood and skilfully piles them up, struggling to stick the branches in the hard earth. Next he feeds the incipient flames with pieces of dry bark. A boy stands by holding a flat basket in his hands. Then when he has thrown three handfuls of corn into the flames, a little girl offers the sliced honeycombs. Others hold the wine; some of each is dedicated to the flames; they look on, and, dressed in white, keep sacred silence. The Terminus who belongs to both properties is sprinkled with the blood of a sacrificed lamb, and raises no objection when he is given a sucking pig. The peasant neighbourhood comes together to celebrate and to chant your praises, sacred Terminus.

Religious bonds linked households together through family relationships; and we may note how often anxieties about competition for scarce resources between close relatives surface in literature (anxieties which were expressed in Greek culture by myths about parent-murder and fratricide, and at Rome by the legend of Romulus and Remus).

### 38  Ovid, *Fasti* 2, 617–34

The following day is called the Caristia, from *cari* – 'dear ones'. A crowd of relatives comes to the gods that are theirs; no doubt it is pleasant to turn our faces away from the tombs and those of our relatives who have died towards those who are alive, and to look at what is left of our kinsfolk after all those we have lost, and count up the levels of kinship.

Let the innocent appear; let a disloyal brother stay far, far away from here, and a mother who is hard on her offspring, anyone who thinks his father is still too much alive, anyone who counts up his mother's years, or the unjust mother-in-law who acts harshly towards her daughter-in-law. . . .

Good people, offer incense for the gods of your clan; Concord will be particularly kind to you on this day. Offer food, so that, pleased at this pledge of respect, the Lares with their tunics girt may feed from the plate you offer them. And when the dewy night invites you to a dream-free sleep, pour out plenty of wine as you pray in these words: 'Good luck to you, Lares, and good luck to you, Caesar, best of men'; these are good words to go with good wine.

The emotional bonds of the Roman household were not just marital and parental. Slaves and freedmen too were expected to identify with the master or patron from whom they derived their material and social existence (without whom the slave could not survive at all, and the freedman or woman would not have become an independent citizen). A humane master like Pliny represented himself as treating his slaves as analogous to citizens. But there is no question of slaves leaving property to anyone of their choice who does not belong to Pliny's household.

### 39  Pliny, *Letters* 8, 16

The incidence of sickness among my slaves has caused me concern; there have been deaths, even among those in their prime. There are two consolations; they cannot cancel out the grief, but they are consolations. One is the ease with which they can be manumitted, for I feel that I have not lost them before their time if I lose them as free men; the other is that I allow even my slaves to make a sort of will, which I respect as if it were legally binding. (2)  They give orders and make requests as they wish, and I obey as though bound by their commands. They divide up their belongings, grant and bequeath (so long as it is within the household): for to slaves the household is a sort of state, a substitute community.

# THE ROMAN HOUSEHOLD

Old family retainers identified closely with their master's fortunes; one was so relieved that his patron's family had survived the regime of Caracalla that he put up the following dedication.

### 40  ILS 3018 = CIL V, 4241 (Concesi, near Brixia, North Italy)

To Jupiter Best and Greatest,
who preserved the property of the Roscian family, of our master Paulus Aelianus of consular rank and of Bassa and of their children. [Set up] in fulfilment of a vow by Lucius Roscius Eubulus, brought up by them (*nutrit*[*us*]; rather than 'who brought them up', *nutrit*[*or*]), their procurator, together with their freedman Publius Roscius Firmus, their procurator. Fourth day before the Nones of March in the consulship of Julianus for the second time and of Crispinus (4 March AD 224).

A freedman might regard his patron and his wife as in a sense part of his own family. The bonds of affection between patron and freedman might resemble those between father and son.

### 41  ILS 4034 = CIL XI, 7485 (Falerii)

Gaius Varius Hermes, to the holy Soranus Apollo; for his own well-being and that of his son and of his patron and of his patron's wife.

Few Romans will have given expression to the patron/freedman relationship in such poetic terms as on the following epitaph from the Via Appia outside Rome. Marcus Aurelius Cotta Maximus Messalinus was the younger son of Tibullus's patron Messalla Corvinus (25, p. 30). A noted orator and a friend of the poet Ovid, he was consul in AD 20 and a leading public figure throughout Tiberius's reign.

### 42  ILS 1949 = CIL XIV, 2298 (Via Appia, Rome)

[Here lies] Marcus Aurelius Zosimus, freedman of Cotta Maximus, his patron's aide-de-camp.

I admit that I was a freedman; but now my shadow has been ennobled by my patron Cotta. Several times he was willing to grant me an equestrian fortune, he ordered me to let my children live so that he could provide for their upkeep. He was always ready to grant me his own wealth. He also gave my daughters the dowries a father provides. He promoted my son Cottanus to the rank of tribune in which he bravely served in Caesar's army. What did Cotta not give us? Now, sadly, he provided these verses which can be read on my tomb.

Aurelia Saturnia, Zosimus's [wife].

> M.Aurelius Cottae Maximi
>   Zosimus, accensus patroni.
> Libertinus eram, fateor: sed facta legetur
>   patrono Cotta nobilis umbra mea.
> Qui mihi saepe libens census donavit equestris
>   qui iussit natos tollere quos aleret
> quique suas commisit opes mihi semper, et idem
>   dotavit natas ut pater ipse meas,
> Cottanumque meum produxit honore tribuni
>   quem fortis castris Caesaris emeruit.
> Quid non Cotta dedit? qui nunc et carmina tristis
>   haec dedit in tumulo conspicienda meo.
>     Aurelia Saturnia, Zosimi.

A very fragmentary inscription from Forum Livi (Forli) in Tuscany illustrates the ideal that a patron should look after both the moral and the material well-being of his freedmen and tenants.

## 43  CIL XI, 600 (Forli)

Gaius Castricius Calvus Agricola, son of Titus, of the Stellatine tribe, the well-wishing patron of good [?farmers or freedmen] – especially of those who [worked hard and] well to cultivate their fields, and [who looked after] their own bodies carefully (the most important requirement [for farmers]); who fed themselves, and [who looked after] whatever possessions they had.

Let anyone who wishes [to live] in a truly good and free fashion [hold these] precepts for true:

The first is that you should want to be loyal [to your lord], respect [your parents and keep] your promises [. . . not win a bad] reputation. A man who does no [harm and keeps his promises] will have a pleasant [and trouble-free life], happily and with a clear conscience.

Agricola teaches you to remember these precepts, which [he did not learn from philosophers, but from] nature and experience.

To Lucius Castricius, freedman of Gaius.
I mourned his death because he deserved it, and [arranged his burial and provided a place;] and I had this memorial made to him so that [all freedmen should have an] incentive to be loyal to their patrons.

Also to Castricia Helena, freedwoman of Gaius, because [she too was loyal.]

One expression of the bonds between patron and ex-slave was the right of a freedman to be buried in the family tomb. Many such inscriptions show how freedmen and *alumni* were thought to be integral members of the household. If a patron was dissatisfied with the degree of respect a freedman had paid him, he might make a provision in his will excluding him from such burial (as in the will of 'Dasumius', **158**, pp. 137f.). This tomb refers to a man of senatorial rank, his *alumnus* (perhaps his natural son, and apparently adopted) and a freedwoman concubine.

## 44  CIL VI, 31665 (Rome)

To Lucius Percennius Lascivus, also called Monnicus, Roman *eques*, dearest *alumnus* and most peerless, most sweet and most beloved son;
Lucius Percennius Pollio, of senatorial family, his parent.
Also Sabina Felicitas, to her most sweet husband and peerless and most loving master.

This inscription names a freedman–husband and his fellow-freedwoman who was apparently the mother of two children born as slaves in the same household and later freed. (Eudoxus was under age and had to be freed with the permission of a council: see **191**, paragraph 19, p. 160). Luria Musa was perhaps Felix's second wife.

### 45   ILS 1984 = CIL XIV, 1437 (Ostia)

Decimus Otacilius Felix made this tomb for himself and
for his co-freedwoman Otacilia Hilara,
for the freedman Decimus Otacilius Hilarus,
for the freedman Decimus Otacilius Eudoxus,
  [later addition] set free before a council
for his wife Luria Musa,
and for all my other freedmen and freedwomen and their descendants, excepting those whom I shall exclude in my will.
Street front: 30 feet. Depth into field: 25 feet.

Freedmen as well as free-born citizens used the ideal of the *domus* to express stability and security – an indication of the success of Augustus's wish that slaves should not be freed unless they had been 'acculturated' with Roman values. An example of emotional solidarity within the *domus* comes from the tomb of the Memmii at Rome (cf. ILS 8341 = Wiedemann, GARS, 49).

### 46   ILS 8432 = CIL VI, 22355a (Rome)

For Aulus Memmius Clarus,
Dedicated by Aulus Memmius Urbanus to his fellow freedman and dearest companion. I cannot remember, my most respected co-freedman, that you and I ever quarrelled. By this epitaph, I invoke the gods of heaven and of the underworld as witnesses that we first met on the slave-dealer's platform, that we were granted our freedom together in the same household, and that nothing ever parted us from one another until the day of your death.

Respect for the family connections of slaves contradicts the principle that a slave-owner could do whatever he wished with his slaves. Consequently the law of the classical period could not recognise any family relationships (e.g., parent/child, husband/wife) among slaves; the only formal relationship they had was with their master. Slaves always had to fear that they might be separated, either as a punishment or if the household to which they belonged were split up. At Puteoli on 5 October AD 51, a number of slaves were sold because they had been used as security for a loan which their master could not repay. Another document in the same dossier (AE 1973, no. 161) shows that this group of slaves was still together and registered as Cinnamus's property on 30 October. (Cf. J. A. Crook, 'Working Notes on some of the New Pompeii Tablets', ZPE 29 (1976), 229–39.)

## 47 AE 1973, no. 139 (Pompeii)

In the consulship of Tiberius Claudius Caesar (for the fifth time) and of Lucius Calventius Vetus, third day before the Nones of October; in the forum at Puteoli; a notice was placed on the square pillar in the Sextian Portico of Augustus, containing the following inscription:

The male slaves Felix, Carus, Januarius; female slaves Primigenia, Primigenia the younger; boy Ampliatus; property of Marcus Egnatius Suavis, which he is said to have given to Gaius Sulpicius Cinnamus by mancipation for 1 sestertius, as security in consideration for a loan of 23 (thousand?) sesterces; these slaves will be put up for sale at Puteoli on 14 October in the forum in front of the Portico of Caesonius. The pledge became forfeit on 15 September.

In late antiquity, the principle that property-rights should take precedence over the bonds of family was humanely modified by the Emperor Constantine (AD 334 or 325).

## 48 *Theodosian Code* 2, 25.1

Who could accept the idea that children should be parted from their parents, sisters from brothers, wives from their husbands? It follows that any person who has parted slaves who are related and taken them off to different owners is to be made to bring these slaves back and leave them in the ownership of the same person. If anyone loses his property in slaves when families are reunited, then the man who receives the slave concerned must indemnify him by giving him another slave in his place. Ensure that there are no complaints from now on about slave families being divided.

# III

# IDEALS AND ANXIETIES

Publilius Syrus's collection of commonplace maxims throws some light on the ideals and anxieties of adult males in the Graeco-Roman world about domestic as well as political or business affairs (for instance, men's fears about losing control over their women). The sentiments expressed are sometimes contradictory, but they illustrate various aspects of domestic life: the importance of economic self-sufficiency (line 11) and of the household as the basic unit of emotional support (182); the role of women, slaves and freedmen; serial monogamy (260, 381); the importance of *amicitiae* (284, 549); and the prevalence of infanticide and violence against the younger generation (see Chapter V).

### 49 Publilius Syrus, *Maxims*

11  Money borrowed is bitter slavery for a free-born man.
108 The housewife who is chaste commands next to her husband by obeying.
123 He who kills a child is cruel, not brave.
124 The master who fears those he commands is their slave.
182 The exile with no home (*domus*) is a dead man without a tomb.
260 Frequent weddings give rise to unpleasant rumours.
284 Behave towards a friend as though you remembered that he could easily become your enemy.
363 A master who fears his slaves is less than a slave.
381 A woman who marries many times displeases many husbands.
498 A good freedman is a son notwithstanding nature.
514 When a parent is angry, he is most cruel towards himself.
534 It is counted as a virtue to do wrong for one's master's sake.

549   The dinner-table can hold more friends than the mind.
627   A young man must be overcome by reason, not force.
659   The grief of a nurse comes next to that of a mother.

An extract from the funeral speech of Lucius Caecilius Metellus, given in 221 BC and preserved by Pliny the Elder, gives us some idea of the moral values which wealthy and politically powerful Roman males accepted as their ideals. Metellus had been consul in 251 and 247 BC, and dictator in 224. We may note that all but two of the ten ideals listed relate to the 'public' rather than the 'private' sphere: citizen women (as well as children and slaves) were automatically excluded from them. It is less clear whether the sentiments expressed were restricted to the elite, or whether ordinary peasant citizens might share them (even if they could themselves not attain many of them).

## 50   Pliny, *Natural History* 7, 43/139–40

He had to his credit ten of the greatest and best achievements which sages spend their lives trying to attain. Namely, he wished to be a warrior of the first rank; an outstanding public speaker; a most courageous general; one who won great military victories under his own auspices; to hold the highest offices; to have great wisdom; to be considered the foremost senator; to acquire a great deal of money in an honest fashion; to leave behind many children; and to be held in great fame in the community. All of these aims were achieved by him, and by no one else since the foundation of Rome.

Inscriptions on tombs can give us some insight into the different virtues that were thought appropriate to young and old, male and female, slave, freed and free. A family tomb at Rome proclaims the obedience expected (or hoped for) from a teenage son and from wives, the harmony between a married couple and the importance of children.

## 51   ILS 8430 = CIL VI, 20158 and 20116 (Rome)

[Dedicated to] Publius Julius Nomaeus, son of Publius, an excellent, respectful and dutiful son. He is master of this whole place (i.e., the tomb); he lived for 15 years, 10 months and 24 days. [Set up by] his father Publius Julius Lysiponus.

Sacred to the Spirits of the Deceased.
To Publius Julius Lysiponus, freedman of the ex-consul Lupus. I lived for seventy-one years; fifteen of them with my first wife Donata, twenty-eight with the lady Rhodine. There was no discord with either of them, both were most obedient to me, and by them I had three male children.

P.Iulio P.[f.] Nomaeo filio optumo reverentissimo obsequentissimoq. huiusq. loci totius domino, vix. ann. XV m. X d. XXIV. P. Iul. L[ysi]ponus pat. d.m.s. P. Iulio Lupi cos. lib. Lysipono qui vixi an. LXXI, quib. cum Donata coniuge prim. an. XV, cum Rhodine domin. an. XXVIII, sine utriusque offens. mihiq. obsequentissimis, e quib. et genui<t> fil. masculos tres.

The longest and most detailed surviving epitaph is conventionally given the title *Laudatio Turiae* ('the eulogy of Turia') because of a suggested identification of the wife with one whose succour of her husband at the time of the triumviral proscriptions, noted by Valerius Maximus (6, 7.2), recalls certain events recounted in the inscription. Events in the first paragraph relate to 49 BC; later on, we learn that the wife's intercession saved her husband in 42 BC. She may have died as late as 2 BC. The text, from Rome, is in the form of a speech, which may actually have been delivered at her funeral. Throughout, her husband addresses her directly. The identities of the couple are unknown (see N. Horsfall, *Bulletin of the Institute of Classical Studies* 30 (1983), 85–98, esp. 91f.), but they were evidently wealthy.

Possession by 'Turia' of the conventional matronly virtues is more or less taken for granted. Other portions of the text show the importance attached to having children (the couple may have suffered under Augustus's marriage legislation) and to equipping unmarried women with dowries. The family solidarity shown by 'Turia' is notable. The 'common housekeeping' of which the husband speaks (lines 37ff.) probably amounted in practice to his administering (*tutela*), with her consent, her private property while she, in her role as housekeeper, looked after (*custodia*) his. It is possible that her father, in his will, had also given him *tutela* in the legal sense, so that his authorisation was needed for certain transactions affecting her property.

*Manus* marriage had not entirely disappeared by this time. The deceased's sister had entered *manus*. So (apparently some considerable time after her marriage) had her mother, by the process known as *coemptio*. This was the basis of the fraudulent claim to *tutela* on grounds of membership of a *gens* (the latest classical example attested). *Coemptio* would have made the mother one of the *sui heredes* (heirs on intestacy) to the father, so invalidating his previous will, since all such *heredes* must either be made heirs or explicitly disinherited. 'Turia' would then have become the sole heir, through intestacy; and the claimants hoped to control the disposal of her fortune.

The Latin text may be found in ILS 8393 = FIRA III no. 69. See M. Durry, *Eloge Funèbre* (Paris, 1950); E. Wistrand, *The So-Called Laudatio Turiae* (Lund, 1976).

## 52 The *Laudatio Turiae* ('Eulogy of Turia')

(Column 1, 1.3) You were suddenly left orphaned [prior] to the day of [our marriage] when both your [parents were mur]dered in a lone[ly country district. It was primarily due to you] that the death of your parents [did not remain unavenged,] since I was [on my way to] Macedonia, and your sister's husband [Gaius Cluvius on his way to] the province of Africa. (7) You put so much effort into performing this sacred [duty by insisting on a prosecution] and due punishment, that we would not have been able to give any further help if we *had* been in a position to help. These achievements you performed together with the revered lady [your sister].

(10)   While you were involved in all this, when punishment had been carried out on those who were guilty, you left your paternal house in order to protect your virtue. You immediately betook yourself to the house of my mother, where you waited for my return. You were then put under pressure to declare that your father's will, in which we were declared the heirs, was invalid, on the grounds that he had taken his wife into *manus* by a *coemptio*.[1] This would have made it necessary for you, together with all your father's property, to revert to the guardianship of those who were making this claim. Nothing would have gone to your sister, because she had passed from the *manus* of your father into that of Cluvius. Although I was not there at the time, I was told about the courage with which you listened to their proposals, and the presence of mind with which you rejected them.

(18) You protected our common interests by stating the truth: (you said that) the will had not been invalidated. In order that [both of us] might hold the inheritance, [rather than] you alone possess the entire property, it was your firm resolve to uphold what your father had done, in the same way that, if you had not won your point, you intended to share with your sister; and you were not going to let yourself pass under the compulsory guardianship[2] of someone who had no legal claim upon you, and for whom no gentile relationship with your own family could be shown to exist, which might force you to do that. Even if your father's will could be declared void, nevertheless that right did not lie with those who claimed it, since they did not belong to the same *gens*.

(25) In the face of your resolution, they gave up, and did not press the matter any further. As a result, all by yourself you successfully carried to a conclusion your defence of your reverence towards your father, your proper feeling towards your sister and your loyalty to me.

(27) Not many marriages last so long to be ended by death rather than broken up by divorce. We were privileged that ours lasted for forty-one years, without argument. I only wish that the final end of the marriage had come about through my own death instead, since it would have been more just for me, as the elder, to yield to fate.

(30) Why [should I mention] the domestic virtues? You were chaste, obedient, sociable, easy to get on with, [diligent] at your wool-working, [respected the gods] without indulging in excessive devotions, were well-dressed without showiness and discreetly elegant. Why should I say anything about your love for your relatives and your devotion to your family, since you looked after my mother in just the same way as your own parents, and ensured the same security for her as for yours? You shared innumerable other qualities with all ladies who strive for a worthy reputation. The qualities which I bear witness to were uniquely yours, and few men have experienced their like, so as to be able to make public and vouch for such qualities, since human destiny has ensured that they are not frequent.

(37) We maintained by our common housekeeping the whole of the inheritance you received from your parents, and you did not want anything more, since you passed it all over to me. We

divided our responsibilities between us in such a way that I bore the guardianship (*tutela*) for your property, and you assisted me in looking after mine. I will not go into detail on this subject in order not to confuse your personal part in this with my own. Let it be enough for me to have drawn attention to your feelings on this subject.

(42) You showed yourself generous both towards your many relatives and especially in the respect you showed your family (*pietas*). One might of course mention others in terms of similar praise, but there was only one who came up to you in this respect [. . .] you had your sister; for your female relatives [worthy (?) . . . (with)] attentions in your own houses, you (plural) brought up at home with us. And you gave dowries to these same girls so that they might attain a state fitting to your family. I and Gaius Cluvius between us decided to pay for these dowries on which you had decided ourselves, so that while giving approval to your liberality we would not let you diminish your own inheritance. So we paid them from our own personal property instead, and provided the dowries out of our own estates. I have mentioned this, not to boast on my own behalf, but so that everyone should know that we considered it an honour to carry out with our own money decisions which you had made out of your piety and generosity. [. . .]

(Column II, line 35) When the world returned to peace and the Republic was restored, then we enjoyed tranquil and [happy] times. We wanted children, which for some [long time Fate] had [begrudged]. If Fortune had complied and allowed things to take their usual course, [what would the two of] us have lacked? The passage of time put an end to hope. [I shall now declare] what [you] urged [because of this] and on [what] course you attempted to embark – behaviour which in certain women would be [perhaps striking and remarkable], but in your case elicits scarcely any admiration in comparison with [the rest of] your virtues.

(41) Doubting your own fertility [and] distressed at my being without children, you spoke of [divorce], so that I should not, by remaining [married] to you, forfeit hope of children and so be rendered [unfortunate]. You offered to [yield the house] to another, fertile, woman, with the [sole] intention of yourself seeking out and providing for me a state of life [worthy] of the

harmony known to exist between us. You declared that you would consider the children as [shared], and [as if] they were your own; and that you would not make any division of our property, [which hitherto] had been common, but that [it] would continue to be [controlled by me] and, if I were willing, looked after by you; you would look on nothing as distinct [or separate]. Henceforth you would render me the services and the affection of a sister or a [mother-in-law].

(50) I must admit that I was so furious that I was beside myself, so [horrified at] your proposal that I could scarcely recover my composure. To think that divorce between us could be discussed [before] Fate had imposed its decree, or that [you] could contemplate anything that [made you cease] to be my wife [while you lived], you who had steadfastly remained loyal when I was almost an exile from life.

*Notes*

1  *Coemptio* was the fictitious sale of a woman (and, in consequence, the actual transfer of her property) into the *manus* of her husband. Since a wife in *manus* was one of a man's heirs on intestacy, the *coemptio* would have invalidated any previous will Turia's father had made. Turia herself was the sole heir on intestacy (since her sister was in her husband's *manus* and her mother dead).
2  *Tutela legitima*, the technical term for the *tutela* that goes automatically to agnates when no alternative provision has been made by a *pater* in his will.

Funeral epitaphs do not necessarily reveal the virtues that women thought important, but they certainly show us what men hoped to find in women.

### 53   ILS 8402 = CIL VI, 11602 (Rome)

Here lies Marcus's (wife) Amymone, the best and most beautiful,
Busy at her wool-working, devoted, modest, thrifty, chaste,
happy to stay at home.

> Hic sita est Amymone Marci optima et pulcherrima,
> lanifica pia pudica frugi casta domiseda.

### 54   ILS 8403 = CIL I, 1007 (Rome; second century BC)

Visitor, what I have to say is not much, stand a moment and read.

This tomb is not beautiful, but it is for a beautiful woman. Her parents gave her the name Claudia. She loved her husband with her whole heart. She bore two children, of whom she left one above ground, and buried the other under the earth. Her conversation was agreeable, her bearing pleasing. She stayed at home, she worked at her wool. I have finished speaking. You may go.

hospes, quod deico, paullum est, asta ac pellege.
Heic est sepulcrum hau pulcrum pulcrai feminae.
Nomen parentes nominarunt Claudiam.
Suom mareitum corde deilexit souo.
Gnatos duos creavit, horunc alterum
in terra linquit, alium sub terra locat.
Sermone lepido, tum autem incessu commodo.
Domum servavit, lanam fecit. Dixi. Abei.

## 55  ILS 8450 = CIL VI, 29580 (Rome)

Sacred to the Spirits of the Deceased.
To Urbana, the sweetest, most chaste and exceptional wife. I am sure that nothing has been more wonderful than her. She deserves to be honoured by this inscription, since she spent her whole life with me utterly joyfully and without complication, with both married affection and with characteristic hard work. I have added these words so that those who read them may understand how deeply we loved one another. Paternus set this up to her who deserved it.

d.m.s. Urbanae coniugi dulcissime et castissimae ac rarissimae, cuius praeclarius nihil fuisse certus, hoc etiam titulo honorari meruit, quae ita mecum cum summa iucunditate adque simplicitate in diem vitae suae egit quam adfectioni coniugali tam industria morum suorum. Haec ideo adieci, ut legentes intellegant, quantum nos dilexerimus. Paternus b.m.f.

Chastity and fidelity was a prime concern.

## 56  ILS 8456 = CIL VI, 34268 (Rome)

To the Spirits of the Deceased Aelia Tryphera,
an exceptional wife, pure and chaste beyond what can be expected

of the average female; she lived for 24 years 7 months 10 days. Aelius Proximus put this up.

d.m. Aeliae Trypherae coniugis rarissimae et ultra modum sexumque muliebrem sanctissimae castissimaeque, quae vix. ann. XXIIII mens. VII d. X, Aelius Proximus posuit.

Another was hard work.

### 57   ILS 8437 = CIL IX, 1913 (Benevento)

To the Spirits of the Deceased Octavia Crescentina,
who lived her life in accordance with the life-style of old, deeply respected for her reliability and hard work. Her husband Gaius Valerius Januarius, with their son(s?), set this up to her who well deserved it.

d.m. Octaviae Crescentinae que antiqua vita viixit, fidei ac diligentiae [gr]aviss., C.Val.Ianuarius coniux c.fil. b.m.f.

### 58   ILS 8444 = CIL VIII, 11294 (near Thelepte, Algeria)

Sacred to the Spirits of the Deceased.
Postumia Matronilla was a wife without peer, a good mother, a dutiful grandmother, modest, pious, hard-working, thrifty, active, wakeful, concerned; she married one man, and slept with one man; she was a matron who worked hard and could be relied upon. She lived for 53 years, 5 months and 3 days.

d.m.s. Postumia Matronilla inconparabilis coniux, mater bona, avia piissima, pudica religiosa laboriosa frugi efficaxs vigilans sollicita univira unicuba [t]otius industriae et fidei matrona, vixit annis n.LIII mensibus n.V diebus tribus.

Hard physical work does not appear in such an explicit form in the epitaphs of ladies of high rank, such as that of Vinicia Marciana, daughter of an equestrian governor and praetorian prefect, and wife of Nonius Verus, consular, governor and patron of many Italian cities, on a fourth-century AD sarcophagus.

IDEALS AND ANXIETIES

## 59  ILS 1218 = CIL XI, 831 (Modena)

To a most reverend and loving wife, whose life was so outstanding for her praiseworthy habits and activities and all the virtues of her character that she surpassed the exemplars of ancient probity. By the judgement of all and their unparalleled commendation, she deservedly was held to be the glory and ornament of all famous matrons.

Coniugi sanctissimae ac benignissimae cuius vita morum studiorumq. laudibus et universis virtutum animi tam clara exstitit ut admirabilia veteris probitatis exempla superarit quo merito omniumque iudicio singulari praeconio inlustrium matronarum decus ornamentumq. est abita.

Then as now, reality will not always have corresponded to the public image of marital harmony which Romans liked to present to the outside world. One of the few documented instances of a family row occurs in a letter of 51 BC written to Atticus by Cicero, whose brother Quintus had married Atticus's sister Pomponia.

## 60  Cicero, *Letters to Atticus* 5, 1.3–4

Let me turn to the question of your sister, which you added in the margin of your last note. This is the position. When I returned to Arpinum, my brother came to see me. First we spoke about you for some considerable time. Then I mentioned the conversation we had about your sister when we were at my estate at Tusculum. On that occasion no one could have been nicer and more conciliatory than my brother was about your sister; if there was a grudge for any reason, it did not surface. So much for that day. Then on the next day we set off from Arpinum. I was on my way to Aquinum; because of the festival, Quintus had to stay at the villa at Arx for the night, and we stopped there for lunch (you know the estate). When we arrived, Quintus said in a perfectly nice way, 'You call the women, Pomponia, and I'll deal with the lads.' To me at least, it seemed totally agreeable – the words, the intention, the manner. She said – in our hearing – 'I myself am just a guest in this house.' Perhaps the real reason why she was upset was that Statius (one of Quintus's slaves rather than

55

Pomponia's) had been sent on ahead to get the meal ready. Quintus said to me: 'You see what I have to put up with all the time?' 'What did it matter?' you may ask. A lot – I was greatly upset myself. Her words and behaviour were uncalled for and rude. I did not show how annoyed I was. We all reclined for lunch, except for her; when Quintus nevertheless had something sent out to her, she sent it back. In sum, I have never seen anyone as restrained as my brother, or as impossible as your sister. I omit several things that upset me more than Quintus at the time. I continued to Aquinum; Quintus stayed at the estate at Arx and came to see me the next morning. He told me that Pomponia had refused to let him sleep with her that night, and that when he left she had behaved just in the way I had seen myself. You may tell her to her face that I think that her behaviour that day was unacceptable.

Valerius Maximus discusses the marital customs of the Romans of old, including the introduction of divorce (on the grounds of infertility) and the (sparing) use of wine and jewellery by women in days when they were virtuous. But even then there had been frictions, and rituals to contain them.

## 61  Valerius Maximus 2, 1.6

Whenever there was some little argument between husband and wife, they used to go to the shrine of the goddess Viriplaca ('man-placater') on the Palatine hill. There each in turn stated what they wanted; and after they had put aside their quarrelsome feelings, they went back home in harmony. The goddess is said to have obtained this name from her power to placate husbands; she certainly deserves to be venerated and honoured with some outstanding and exceptional sacrifices, as the guardian of peace in everyday and household affairs, who by her very title grants the respect owed by wives to the superior rank of husbands within the yoke of equal affection.

The *paterfamilias* had the right to control his wife in the same way as his children only if she had transferred from the *potestas* of her father into her husband's *manus* at marriage (in fact, few marriages in the historical period involved such a transfer; most wives remained under the *potestas* of their fathers until the latter died). The prevalence of 'free' marriage meant that wives were to some extent protected from suffering violence at the hands of their husbands (though not all husbands behaved as they should; Tacitus mentions a praetor who threw his wife out of a window, though he subsequently committed suicide: *Annals* 4, 21). But notwithstanding the legal independence of wives, some Roman writers liked to represent the absolute authority of husbands as right and proper. (On the control of wine-drinking by women, note also Pliny, *Natural History* 14.12f.: the praetor Gnaeus Domitius awards *dos* to a husband because his wife has drunk more wine than is necessary for her health.)

## 62  Valerius Maximus, 6, 3.9

Egnatius Maecenius killed his wife by beating her with a stick for being drunk on wine. Not only was he not summoned to court for doing this, but he was not even criticised by anyone: all right-thinking men considered that she deserved what she got because of her lack of self-control. It is agreed that any woman who drinks without restraint puts any virtue she may have at risk and risks falling prey to every vice.

Notwithstanding the ideal of life-long marriage, divorce and remarriage was frequent, at least among the wealthy senatorial families of the late Republic and early Empire.

## 63  Suetonius, *Augustus* 62

As a young man, Augustus had been betrothed to the daughter of Publius Servilius Isauricus, but after his first disagreement with Mark Antony had been made up, and the soldiers of their two armies insisted that they be brought together by means of some kind of marriage alliance, he took Antony's step-daughter Claudia (the daughter of Fulvia and of Publius Clodius) as his wife, although she was barely old enough for marriage. Then there was a quarrel with his mother-in-law Fulvia, so he sent Claudia away without having slept with her, still a virgin. Then he married Scribonia, who had previously been the wife of two ex-consuls, and had even borne one of them a child. He divorced her as well, 'tired of the perversity of her habits' (as he himself wrote), and immediately took Livia Drusilla away from her husband Tiberius Nero, although she was pregnant, and loved and respected her alone throughout the rest of his life.

Plutarch's account of affairs in the 'women's quarters' (*gynaikonitis*) of Cato the Younger's household shows that in the first century BC, women of the elite had considerable freedom to live the love-life they wished; consequent divorce may not have been too high a price to pay. But at the same time, the story that Cato handed his wife over to Hortensius (coloured by themes from Greek philosophy, and disbelieved by Plutarch himself) suggests that men could still see their wives and daughters as instruments for child-bearing, whose emotions hardly needed to be taken account of when political marriage-alliances were being considered.

### 64  Plutarch, *Cato the Younger* 24–5

24 (4)  Cato's womenfolk seem to have been a total disaster. One sister was rumoured to be having an affair with Caesar. Cato's other sister Servilia behaved even more disgracefully. Having married Lucullus, one of the greatest Romans of the time, and borne him a child, she was thrown out of his house for her sexual indiscretions. Worst of all, not even Cato's own wife Atilia was free of such immorality. Although he had two children by her, he felt it necessary to divorce her for her shamelessness.

25 (1)  He went on to marry Philippus's daughter Marcia, apparently an honourable woman, about whom a particularly curious story is told. This episode is as inexplicable and extraordinary as a soap opera. Thraseas, following the account of Cato's friend and associate Munatius, tells the story as follows. (2) Some of Cato's many friends and admirers were more famous and well-known than others, including Quintus Hortensius, a man of outstanding fame and character. Wanting to be more than just a friend and companion to Cato, but also to become as closely joined to him as possible and to link their two households and families, he tried to persuade him to give him his daughter Porcia, who was living with Bibulus and had borne him two sons, since

she had proved fertile ground for offspring. (3) This sort of thing was absurd in people's eyes, but it was noble in the eyes of nature and politically expedient that a woman in the prime of life should neither have her productive capacity limited nor by having more children than was necessary bring burdens and beggary upon a household that did not want them. If worthy men had successors in common, then no one would be jealous of the virtue that would multiply in their families, and their relationships would tie the community ever more closely together. If Bibulus was too fond of his wife, then he would give her back to him as soon as she had borne a child. Thus he would be closely related both to Bibulus and to Cato through children they would share.

(4) Cato replied that he loved Hortensius and liked the idea of sharing a family relationship with him, but thought it ridiculous to talk about marrying his daughter, who had already been given to someone else. So Hortensius used a different approach and asked Cato straight out for his own wife, who was still young enough to have children, on the grounds that Cato already had enough heirs. (5) It cannot be said that he did this because he thought that Cato was not fond of Marcia; it is said that she was pregnant at the time. Cato saw how keen Hortensius was, and could not think of any objections; but he said that Marcia's father Philippus would have to give his approval. Philippus was consulted and agreed, but would only give Marcia away in Cato's own presence and with his participation.

Divorce and remarriage resulted in a significant number of children having step- and half-brothers and sisters. The law codes of most northern European countries since the nineteenth century assign the custody of children in the case of their parents' divorce to the mother; but since in Roman law the *potestas* of a father over his legitimate children was unquestioned, the children of divorced parents at Rome would normally be expected to remain with him. Also, Roman law had to deal with possible disagreements about responsibility for children born after a divorce. Any such child acknowledged as legitimate would have a claim upon the father's property.

**65** *Digest* **25, 3.1 (Ulpian,** *On the Edict,* **book 34)**

(1) If a woman believes herself pregnant, she, or the parent in whose *potestas* she is, or a person instructed by them, may announce the fact within thirty days, reckoning from the divorce, to the husband himself or the parent in whose *potestas* he is, or to their house, if neither person is available. . . .

(3) The woman merely gives notice of her pregnancy, but not for the purpose of having her husband send persons to keep watch on her. It is sufficient that the woman notifies the fact of her pregnancy. It is up to the husband either to send observers or to declare that she is not pregnant by him, and this he may do either personally or through someone else. The husband is penalised if he does not either send observers or, on the other hand, expressly deny that she is pregnant by him, by being compelled to acknowledge as his the child that is born. . . .

(5) It should be noted that the declaration is initiated by the wife, not by the husband; (6) but if the husband voluntarily offers observers and she refuses to admit them, or if the wife makes no declaration, or, after making a declaration, refuses to admit the observers appointed by a court, it is open to the husband or his parent not to recognise the child.

From the time of Antoninus Pius, there are indications that a divorced mother could appeal to a magistrate to allow her child to stay with her, even if the father had proved that he had *potestas* over the child (see Gardner, WIRLAS, 146–7 and references at note 25).

**66** *Digest* **43, 30.3, 5–6 (Ulpian,** *On the Edict,* **book 71)**

However, even if the father proves that the son is in his *potestas*, nevertheless when the case is heard the mother will be adjudged the preferable person to retain custody, and this is contained in certain decrees of the Deified Pius; for it was granted to a mother, because of the wicked character of the father, that, without detracting from the father's *potestas*, the son should remain with her. In this interdict, the praetor instructs that, pending judgment of the case, a female (child), an under-age male, and one next in age (i.e., just past puberty) should be placed meantime with the *materfamilias*.[1]

# IDEALS AND ANXIETIES

*Note*

1 Glossed as meaning 'a woman of recognised authority (*notae auctoritatis*)'.

### 67 *Code of Justinian* 5, 25.3

The Deified Brothers (Marcus Aurelius and Lucius Verus) To Tatiana, 17 February (?) AD 162.

If you can prove to the appropriate judge that the child whom you say you bore to Claudius is the latter's son, then the judge will order maintenance to be provided for him in accordance with (Claudius's) means. He will also determine whether the child ought to be brought up in Claudius's home.

It was perhaps in order to prevent their children from being looked after by step-mothers, or possibly to avoid having a second legitimate family, and excessively dividing the inheritance, that some men chose not to remarry; they preferred to live with a concubine, often one of their freed-women. An early first-century BC inscription mentions a freedman, his formal wife (once slave of the same master) and another woman with whom he probably lived after the death of his wife; she is described as his freedwoman and concubine (cf. Gardner, WIRLAS, p. 58).

### 68 CIL I(2), p. 729 = ILLRP 795 (Rome)

The copyist (*librarius*) Publius Quinctius, freedman of Titus:
Quinctia, freedwoman of Titus, his wife;
Quinctia Agate, freedwoman of Publius, his concubine.
This tomb is not to pass to outside heirs.

Marcus Aurelius was said not to have remarried, 'so as not to put a step-mother over all his children' (*Historia Augusta*, Marcus 29 *finis*). Cf. Suetonius, *Vespasian* 3 and *Domitian* 12 on imperial concubines. An inscription confirms that Antoninus Pius lived with a concubine (*Historia Augusta*, Pius 8).

61

### 69   ILS 1836 = CIL VI, 8972 (near Rome)

[. . .] Narcissus, freedman of Augustus,
[. . .] a Parthian by origin, *paedagogus* of the emperor's children
and daddy (*papas*) of Galeria Lysistrate, freedwoman of
Augustus, the concubine of the Deified Pius.

At his own expense he rebuilt this [. . .] of the Paelignian
estate, and surrounded it with a wall which he had constructed
from its foundations.

A famous literary account confirms what constituted an ideal wife in the
eyes of one husband. When Pliny the Younger married his third wife
Calpurnia, he was in his mid-forties and had held the consulship; she was
in her teens.

### 70   Pliny, *Letters* 4, 19.2–4

My wife is sensible and careful with our money. She also loves
me, a sign of her virtue. Because of her love for me, she has even
gone so far as to take an interest in literature; she possesses copies
of my writings, reads them repeatedly and even memorises them.
When I am preparing to speak in a lawsuit, she is anxious on my
behalf; when I have completed a case, she is relieved. She sends
out slave messengers to tell her whether I am getting the sympathy
and applause of the jury, and whether the verdict goes my way.
When I recite from my works, she will sit nearby, behind a
curtain, eager to share the praise I receive. She has even set some
of my poems to music, and chants them to the accompaniment of
a lyre, untaught by any music-teacher, but rather by the best of
teachers, love.

Failure to ensure a satisfactory marriage for one's daughter was one of
the signs that a man failed to be a good *paterfamilias*.

### 71   Seneca, *On Benefits* 4, 27.5

A man who engages his daughter to someone who is abusive who has already been divorced several times is looking after his daughter very badly; a man who entrusts his patrimony to someone whom a court has found guilty of business mismanagement will be considered a bad head of household (*malus paterfamilias*); and a man is mad who in his will institutes as his son's tutor someone who has stolen the property of his wards.

We can only speculate on the extent to which the family ideals of the citizen community were shared by others. They were certainly shared by those freedmen whose views have been preserved on inscriptions – but they were by definition those who integrated successfully.

A first- or second-century AD inscription from Villeneuve in the territory of Aosta, set up in memory of his parents and grandparents by a legionary who presumably died on service at Mainz, shows how a man of slave descent could be a respected citizen and *duumvir* (chief magistrate) of his city (cf. the Emperor Pertinax, whose father was reputed to have been born as a slave).

## 72  CIL V, 6896 (Villeneuve)

Quintus Petillius Saturninus, son of Quintus, soldier of the Twenty-Second Legion Primigenia, member of the Board of Six Priests of Augustus, aedile, duumvir; requested in his will that this memorial be set up in accordance with the plans made by Quintus Petillius Syrus, freedman of Quintus;

to his grandfather Quintus Petillius Eros;

his grandmother Petillia Fausta, freedwoman of Quintus;

his father Quintus Petillius Clemens, member of the Board of Six Priests of Augustus;

Lucius Petillius Martialis, his brother;

Salvia Lasciva, his wife.

One of the virtues emphasised on inscriptions was financial independence; both as the peasant virtue of thrift (especially highly regarded in women), but also the citizen virtue of maintaining one's independence by avoiding debt.

## 73  ILS 8436 = CIL VI, 8012 (Rome)

Set up by Gaius Gargilius Haemon, the *paedagogus* and freedman of Proculus the son of Philagrus Agrippianus the freedman of Augustus; a man of reverence and sanctity. I lived for as long as I could, without any lawsuits, arguments or conflicts, and without incurring debts; my friends could trust me; my purse was poor, but my mind rich indeed. Good luck to whoever reads this my inscription.

Obedience was one of the main virtues which parents were anxious to see in their children, whether young or already adult. A Roman inscription cut in rough lettering on cheap stone was put up by a poor family to commemorate two boys who died in an epidemic (on the text, see F. B. R. Hellems, 'The Pupus Torquatianus Inscription: Paleographical Notes', *American Journal of Archaeology* 3 (1899), 202–11, with an illustration).

## 74  ILS 8473 = CIL VI, 27556 (Rome)

Sacred to the Spirits of the Deceased.
The doll (*pupus*) Torquatianus, a good boy who always obeyed his parents (*semper parentibus obsequens*), lived for 8 years 9 months and 13 days; and Laetianus, another doll, also a good boy who obeyed his parents, lived for 5 years 6 months and 6 days. Their parents Gaianus and Eucharis set this up for their sweet sons; but they did not deserve this from you (sc. that the children should have died before their parents). They fell ill on 11 September; one of them lived until 21 September, the other until the 29th of the same month.

Occasionally an inscription allows us to compare directly the feelings that a son was expected to have towards father and mother. While a father was kind to his son (*benignissimus*), a mother was loved by the son (*carissima*). Maxentius was the later emperor (AD 306–12); his son Valerius Romulus, who put up these epitaphs to his parents, actually predeceased him.

## 75   ILS 666–7 = CIL XIV, 2825–6 (Rome)

To my Lord father
Marcus Valerius Maxentius
of senatorial status
Valerius Romulus (boy of
senatorial rank)
out of love
for his affection
[dedicated] to a benevolent
father

To my Lady mother
Valeria Maximilla
of equestrian status
Valerius Romulus (boy of
senatorial rank)
out of love
for her tenderness
[dedicated] to a beloved
mother

A free woman's loyalties were expected to be directed towards her parents and husband; a slave or freedwoman had divided loyalties.

## 76   ILS 8417 = CIL I, 1479 (Cartagena, Spain)

Plotia, the freedwoman of Lucius Plotius and of Fufia. This serving-girl was commonly called Phryne. Here she lies. This monument shows how (well) she behaved towards her ex-master and ex-mistress and her parent and her husband. Farewell, Phryne; and may you (passer-by) fare well.

Plotia L. et Fufiae l. Prune haec voc[i]tatast ancilla heic sitast. Haec qualis fuerit contra patronum patronam parentem coniugem, monumentum indicat. Salve. Salvos seis.

Patience was a primary virtue of any woman, but especially one who was or had been a slave.

## 77   ILS 8422 = CIL VI, 7595 (Rome)

Marcus Claudius Philargyrus,
Freedman of Marcus.
[also]
Plotia Thalassa, freedwoman of Gaius.
She was never sharp
towards her men or her friends.

M.Claudius M.l. Philargyrus. Plotia C.l. Thalassa, viris suis et amicis amara fuit numquam.

For a slave-woman, obedience came first. This inscription suggests that it was expected by her father and her partner as well as her owner.

### 78  ILS 8438 = CIL X, 26 (Locri, South Italy)

Sacred to the Spirits of the Deceased.
[Here lies] Alimma, who during her life served as a slave with total self-control. She lived for 31 years 4 months. With her master's permission, her devoted father and her fellow-slave (set this up) to a most respectful and worthy woman.

d.m.s. Alimma quae in vita sua summa discipulina servavit, vix. ann. XXXI m.IIII, cui de permissu domini fecerunt pater karissimus et conservus pientissimae benemerenti.

Epitaphs listing the characteristics expected of a woman continued to be erected up to the end of antiquity to advertise the virtue and success of the elite. The following verses, inscribed on a marble statue base now in the Capitoline Museum, celebrate Aconia Fabia Paulina, for forty years the wife of a leading late Roman pagan senator. Her husband Vettius Agorius Praetextatus (c. AD 320–84) was the holder (as his monument boasts) of a long list of pagan priesthoods. In addition he was 'in public life quaestor-designate, urban praetor, governor of Tuscany and Umbria, consular governor of Lusitania, proconsul of Achaea, prefect of the city; five times ambassador representing the senate; praetorian prefect of Italy and Illyricum twice; designated ordinary consul'.

### 79  ILS 1259 = CIL VI, 1779 (Rome)

*Right side*:
Vettius Agorius Praetextatus, to his wife Paulina.

Paulina, careful of truth and of honour, dedicated to temples and friend of the gods, who put her husband before herself and Rome before her husband; chaste, faithful, pure in mind and body, kind to all and serviceable to the household gods [. . . *several lines missing . . .*].

*Rear of the base*:
The glory of my own parents gave me no greater gift than that I have seemed worthy of my husband; but all fame and honour is in my husband's name – you, Agorius, born from a proud stock, were a light to your country, to the Senate and to your spouse, with your upright mind, your habits and your culture, with which you attained the highest eminence. For you read whatever was composed in Latin or Greek, whether the thought of wise men for whom the gate of heaven stands open, or the verses which skilled poets have composed, or prose writings; you took it, and improved on it. But these are small things. . . . (*She lists the pagan mysteries into which she had been initiated at her husband's instance.*) By the gift of the mysteries, husband, you freed me, pure and chaste, from the fate of death; you led me into the temples and dedicated me to the gods as their handmaid; with you testifying on my behalf, I was initiated into all mysteries; you, holy husband, honoured me with the sacrifice of bulls as a priestess of Cybele and of Attis; you taught me the triple secret as Hecate's servant, you prepared me for the rites of Greek Demeter. Because of you, all hail me as blessed and holy, because you yourself proclaim me throughout the world as a good woman; I am known to all, even those who do not know me. Why should I not be pleasing, with a husband such as you? Romulus's mothers take me as their example, and think their children fine, if they are like you. Both men and women hope for and approve the ritual garments you put on as master. Now you have laid them aside, and I your wife am grief-stricken and sad. I would have been happy if the gods had granted my husband to survive me; nevertheless I am happy because I am yours, I have been yours and soon, when I am dead, I will be yours.

# IV

# THE ECONOMICS OF THE
# ROMAN HOUSEHOLD

One of the ideals of the ancient city-state was that full citizens should have enough economic independence to play their part in public life without being subject to pressure from others. Those who were really free were expected to own so much productive land that they could afford the leisure for full participation in active politics. Ideally every household was economically self-sufficient; and that 'autarchy' applied not just to production, but also to the provision of services. A *dominus*'s freedom was felt to be curtailed if he had to go outside his household to hire someone with a particular skill, whether a plumber or a physician. In the words of the *Rule of St Benedict* (ch. 66), 'If it can be done, the monastery ought to be so constructed that everything necessary is there within it: water, a mill, a (vegetable) garden, a bakery, and the exercise of different crafts.'

That ideal conflicted with the fact that Roman Italy had a sophisticated money economy; as Roman agricultural textbooks point out, it could be cheaper to buy necessities in the market-place than physically to bring them from a distant part of one's household estates. An efficient network of local roadways could be created only with a massive investment of time and labour – conditions rarely present in antiquity (though the security of the first century AD does seem to have led to considerable building of secondary roads: see T. W. Potter, *The Changing Landscape of South Etruria* (London, 1979), pp. 105–9).

## 80 Varro, *Agriculture* 1, 16.2–6

(2) Farms which have convenient routes for transporting produce to the market-place, and for transporting necessities from the market to the farm, are profitable for that reason. For many landlords include among their estates some to which grain or wine or some other commodity which they do not produce

has to be brought; and on the other hand, not a few landlords own estates which produce something that has to be marketed. (3) So in the vicinity of Rome it is a good idea to go in for large-scale market gardening, and plant violets and roses and all those things which the city will buy; but it is not a good idea to grow these things on a distant estate, where there is no market to take them. Similarly, if there are towns or villages nearby, or even just well-stocked fields and estates belonging to wealthy owners, so that you will be able to buy cheaply from them anything that you need for your own farm, and can sell them your surplus products (e.g., stakes or reeds), then your farm will be more profitable than if these things have to be brought from a long distance. Often it will even be more economical than if you are able to provide these goods yourself by having them produced on your own estate. (4) It is for this reason that smallholders prefer to have a yearly contract with people who live nearby such as physicians, fullers or carpenters, so that they can call on their services, rather than keep men with these skills on their estates – for the death of a single craftsman can often destroy the farm's profitability. On the other hand rich landlords generally entrust all these different functions of a great estate to members of their own household. If towns or villages are too far from their farm, they make sure that they have some smiths and other essential craftsmen in residence on the estate, so that the slaves on the farm will not have to stop work and stay idle as though it was a holiday when something goes wrong, instead of making the estate more profitable by getting on with their tasks. (5) Hence Saserna's handbook[1] prescribes that no one should leave the farm except the manager and the store-keeper and one other, selected by the manager; if anyone else leaves, he should be punished; and if this happens, the manager too should be dealt with. The rule should rather be, that no one should leave the farm without the manager's permission, and that without the owner's express permission the manager himself should not go further from the farm than would allow him to return the same day, nor more frequently than farm business requires. (6) Access to transport makes the same farm more profitable, whether roads along which carts can easily be driven, or adjacent rivers suitable for boats. We know that goods are brought to and from many estates by both these means.

*Note*

1 Saserna: two agricultural writers (father and son) in the first century BC.

When disaster struck, a *dominus* ideally repaired the situation by calling solely on the resources of his own household or 'friends'. In the comedy *Rudens* ('The Rope'), Plautus takes pains to let the audience know that Sceparnio is Daemones' bought slave.[1]

## 81 Plautus, *Rudens* 83–8, 96–102

*Sceparnio:* By all the gods, what a storm Neptune sent us last night! the wind uncovered the villa – it can't be described. It wasn't wind, it was like Euripides' 'Alcmena', the way it blew all the tiles off the roof. It certainly brightened up the place – there are a lot more skylights. . . . (96) Now if I have any sense, I will start preparing the clay, if it kills me.
*Daemones*: I say, Sceparnio!
*Sceparnio*: Who proclaims my name?
*Daemones*: He who paid for you.
*Sceparnio*: You talk as though I were your slave, Daemones.
*Daemones*: We need lots of clay, dig up a lot of earth. I think that the whole villa has to be re-tiled, for it has more holes than a sieve right now.

*Note*

1 On the master's right to decide on his slave's name, see Varro, *On the Latin Language* 8, 9.21 = Wiedemann, GARS, 13; and a passage from the first-century BC jurist Alfenus, *Digest* 35, 1.28.1.

The principle that a *dominus* could supply all his household's needs and services from his own produce and his own labour-force was an ideal that could not be realised by any but the very richest Romans. In fact, even elite households often needed to hire or borrow labour, such as the team of eight litter-bearers that Catullus falsely claimed to have acquired in Bithynia (poem 10). Cicero had to ask Atticus to lend him specialists such as copyists and architects, and there are many references to physicians being 'lent' to friends. (See Chapter VIII for the role of 'friends' in providing such additional support.)

More frequently, requirements for land, housing (e.g., flats such as that leased by Caelius: Chapter I, **9**), and extra services or labour were hired: such hiring agreements were naturally prone to litigation, and many examples are discussed in *Digest* 19, 2 (*locati conducti*). Seneca lists the sorts of things that might be hired.

## 82   Seneca, *On Benefits* 7, 5.2

I have leased a house from you; both you and I have certain rights over it – the property is yours, but the use of your property is mine. In the same way you are not allowed to touch crops, even though they are growing on your property, if your tenant forbids you to do so – and if the price of grain goes up or there is a famine, then 'In vain will you gaze on another's rich harvest'.[1] It grew on your land, it was gathered on your land, it is going to be stored in your granary. Nor are you allowed to come on to land which I have rented, even if you are the owner; nor can you summon away your own slave if I have hired him. If I have hired a carriage from you, then I will be doing you a favour if I allow you to sit down in your own carriage.

*Note*

1   Virgil, *Georgics* 1, 158.

## 83   Varro, *Agriculture* 1, 17

(2)   All fields are worked by human beings, whether slaves or free men or both; they are worked by free men either when these people work their own land, as many poor people do with the help of their children, or when they are hired labourers, as when major agricultural operations such as the vine harvest or hay cutting are undertaken by means of the hired labour of free men; and also by those persons whom the Romans used to call 'debt-bondsmen' (*obaerati*), of whom there are large numbers even today in Asia and Egypt and Illyricum. (3) My view on these people is as follows: it is better to work unhealthy land with hired labourers than with slaves, and even in healthier districts, for large-scale agricultural operations like bringing in the produce of the vintage or the grain harvest. As regards the kinds of qualifications these people should have, Cassius[1] writes:

You should hire labourers who are able to put up with hard work, not less than 22 years old and quick to learn the work of the farm. You can assess this on the basis of how they carried out their previous duties, or by asking those of them who are newly engaged what they had been accustomed to do for their previous employer.

*Note*

1   Gaius Cassius of Utica in North Africa, who wrote an agricultural handbook in the early first century BC.

In terms of time, the greatest single task that had to be performed in any Roman household was the provision of clothing. The importance of preparing yarn was symbolised by the fact that at formal marriage ceremonies, the bride carried a spindle. Augustus publicised the fact that even the women of his family learnt to spin (Chapter V **119**, p. 102). Inscriptions emphasise application to wool-working as one of the virtues men looked for in women (Chapter III **52–4**, pp. 50, 52f.). The same goddess who taught children literature also taught girls the work that would fill much of their lives.

## 84   Ovid, *Fasti* 3, 817–20

After Pallas Minerva has been placated, then girls may begin to learn carding and lighten distaffs full of wool. Pallas is also the goddess who teaches weaving with warp and woof, and pushes the loose warp up with the comb.

The contrast between the subservience in which Roman males liked to picture their womenfolk and the reality was fertile ground for rhetorical attacks on the immorality of women of the elite.

## 85   Columella 12, Preface

(7)   Among the Greeks, and later among the Romans up to the time which our own fathers could remember, almost all work in the household was done by the women, with the heads of

households leaving all their cares behind them and returning to their own homes as though to recuperate from the strains of public life. For there was then total respect, harmony and diligence, and even the most attractive woman burned with the competitive spirit, wishing to make her husband's affairs increase and prosper by her own efforts. (8) Nothing could be seen in the house which was not jointly owned, nothing which either the husband or the wife could legally claim as their personal property; they acted in co-operation, so that the wife's work counted for as much as the husband's public business. So they had no great need for either a manager or a manageress, since the master and the mistress themselves superintended and examined their affairs day by day. (9) But now most women have given themselves up to luxury and idleness to such an extent that they do not even bother to concern themselves with wool-working and disdain clothes produced within the household. They perversely prefer clothes bought for enormous sums of money, indeed almost entire incomes. It is not at all surprising that these women find looking after farms and their workforce irksome, and think that it is quite dreadful to have to spend a few days on a country estate.

Legal sources show that Romans distinguished between two categories of slave work, broadly domestic service and 'rural' production (not just agriculture, but all those industries or crafts required to keep production going).

## 86 Digest 32, 99 (Paul, *On the Meaning of the Word 'Equipment': de significatione instrumenti*)

When 'urban slaves' have been specified in a legacy, some authorities distinguish property in urban slaves not by place, but by the type of work done, so that even if they are on a rural estate, they are considered to be urban slaves so long as they do not do rural work. It should also be said that any slaves whom the head of the household habitually listed among his urban slaves, should be considered as urban slaves; this can most effectively be checked by looking at the household accounts or at the ration list (*ex libellis familiae item cibariis*).

(1)   Doubts may arise as to whether slaves used for hunting or fowling should be included among the urban or the rural slaves. They should be listed as belonging wherever the head of the household had maintained and fed them.

(2)   Mule-drivers perform an urban service, unless the testator had allocated them specifically to work in the country.

(3)   Some legal experts think that a slave who is the child of a slave woman who belongs to the urban group, but was sent to an estate in the country to be brought up, cannot be said to come under either heading. We should rather consider that he belongs to the urban group, for that seems more appropriate.

Ancient agricultural handbooks concentrate on the management of the rural workforce, but the Benedictine rule (although concerned with a productive rural monastery) mentions some of the more responsible services that needed to be performed in any urban household. It emphasises the role of the cellarer, who keeps the stores (ch. 31), and specifies brothers whose job it is to look after iron tools, clothes and other property (ch. 32). Particularly important is the role of the door-keeper (cf. Seneca *Letters* 12, **109**, p. 95).

### 87   *Rule of St Benedict*, ch. 66

Some wise old man should be stationed at the gate of the monastery who is able to take questions and give answers, and whose age will not allow him to go astray (sc. if females appear at the gate). The porter should have his room near the door, so that those who arrive may always find someone present to give them an answer. If this porter is lonely, he can have a younger brother to keep him company.

Slavery enabled a Roman master to perform through the agency of the men he owned actions he could not carry out directly. A master was responsible for his slave's actions, though in certain cases the principle of noxal surrender allowed him to repudiate his slave as culpable (*noxius*) and abandon him to someone who claimed to have been harmed by the slave. But the advantages, for the master, were manifold. For instance, if he did not have a good enough memory, the slave-owner could acquire additional capacity by having his slaves appropriately trained: Calvisius Sabinus was reported by Seneca to have trained a gang of slaves to memorise the Greek classics (*Letter* 27.5f. = Wiedemann, GARS, 132).

Slaves could act as agents for their owner in business deals, making valid contracts with a third party on his behalf; the *Digest* (14, 3) discusses legal actions resulting from obligations entered into by such agents (*institores*).[1] Several such cases are recorded in the dossier of wax tablets found at Murecine, near Pompeii. Here Novius Cypaerus appears to have provided storage facilities for foodstuffs, which Evenus had received from a third party, Eunus, as security for a loan.[2] The whole transaction is handled by the slaves of Cypaerus and Evenus (himself an imperial freedman). The tablet is dated 2 July, AD 37.

## 88  AE 1973, no. 143 (Pompeii)

In the consulship of Gaius Caesar Germanicus Augustus and of Tiberius Claudius Nero Germanicus, on the 6th day before the Nones of July.

I Diognetus, the slave of Gaius Novius Cypaerus, have written on the order of my master that in his presence I have rented to Hesicus, the slave of Primianus Evenus, freedman of Tiberius Julius Augustus, warehouse 12, of the central Bassian warehouses, community property of the people of Puteoli, in which is stored wheat imported from Alexandria which he has received as a pledge today from Gaius Novius Eunus; also in the same warehouse, on the bottom floor, a space between the columns where he has stored 200 sacks of vegetables which he has received from the same Eunus as a pledge from the Kalends of July for one sestertius (*nummus sestertius*) per month.

Done at Puteoli.

*Notes*

1  Not all *institores* were slaves; *filii*, freedmen or even extraneous persons could fulfil this function.
2  Three other tablets, AE 1972, nos 86–8, record a series of loans by Evenus to Eunus totalling 14,130 sesterces. The first two give detailed lists of the foodstuffs Eunus pledges as security. Cf. L. Casson, 'The Role of the State in Rome's Grain Trade', in J. H. D'Arms and E. C. Kopff (eds), *The Seaborne Commerce of Ancient Rome* (Rome, 1980), esp. 26–9.

Slaves might provide services from a very young age: even young children could carry messages, or fetch things. For legal purposes, such as when reckoning up the total value of a dead man's estate, slave children were reckoned to be productive from the age of 5.

### 89 *Digest* 7, 7.6 (Ulpian, *On the Praetor's Edict*, book 55)

When we are dealing with the labour of a slave craftsman, payment has to be in accordance with value; but in the case of unskilled slaves, according to their functions. The jurist Mela agrees.

(1) If the slave is not yet 5 years old or unfit, or in some other way unable to provide his master with labour, then no reckoning of value is made.

(2) Similarly it is impossible to reckon the sentimental or pleasure value of a slave, if for example the master was fond of him or included him among his child pets.[1]

(3) Otherwise the reckoning is to proceed, excluding necessary expenses.

*Note*
1 *In deliciis*: see **124–7** below, pp. 105–7.

### 90 Code of Justinian 6, 43.1 (AD 531)

The value of male and female slaves over 10 years old, if they have no skill, should be assessed at 20 solidi, that of those younger than 10 at no more than 10 solidi; if they are craftsmen, they may be assessed at up to 30 solidi, whether they are male or female, with the exception of secretaries and physicians of either sex. We want secretaries to be valued at 50 solidi, and doctors and midwives at 60. Eunuchs under 10 are worth up to 30 solidi, older ones up to 50; if they have also learnt a craft, up to 70.

Ideally, slaves were brought up and spent their lives in the same household in which they had been born; such a slave was called a *verna*. But in practice many slaves, like other household requirements, had to be bought from outside (cf. Martial's disparaging reference to the slave market, **124**, p. 106). And few households will have been able to undertake the education and training of their *vernae* (like Atticus': 7). Arrangements to have slaves trained in a skill outside the household could lead to litigation.

## 91  *Digest* 17, 1.26.8 (Paul, *On the Praetor's Edict*)

At a friend's formal request (*mandatum*), a smith bought a slave for 10 (sc. gold pieces), taught him his trade, and then sold him for 20, which he was obliged to pay back to the mandator by the terms of the request. Subsequently, on the grounds that the slave was mad, (the smith) was condemned to reimburse the purchaser. The jurist Mela says that the mandator does not have to recompense him (the smith), unless the slave began to suffer from this defect after he had bought him, with no guilty intent on his part. But if the smith had trained the slave on the mandator's formal instructions, then he could demand back both the slave's cost and his upkeep, unless he had asked the smith to train him free.

Landowners were much concerned with the question whether agricultural work could best be undertaken by slaves or by free tenants (*coloni*), who leased parcels of land (normally for periods of five years at a time), which they worked with their own families, sometimes including slaves.

## 92  Columella 1, 7

(3) I myself remember how as an old man Publius Volusius, an extremely wealthy ex-consul, used to say that the most fortunate farm was one whose tenants were local people who had been born there and effectively inherited the place and stayed there because they had been familiar with it right from their childhood. So I believe unreservedly that frequent changes of tenancy are bad for a farm; but renting to a tenant who lives at Rome and prefers to have the land cultivated by his slaves rather than by himself is worse. (4) Saserna (see **80** n. 1, p. 70) used to say that you would get lawsuits rather than rents from this sort of tenant; and that is why we should be careful that if we cannot farm the estate ourselves or through our own slaves, our tenants should be rural

people and not change over too often. But this should only happen in areas where no one wants to live because of a bad climate or infertile soil. (5) If the climate is only moderately healthy, and the soil moderately fertile, then you will always get a higher return from an estate that you look after yourself than from tenants – and you will even get a higher return if it is looked after by a manager, unless he is a particularly incompetent or corrupt slave. And if he does suffer from either of these characteristics, there can be no doubt that it is a mistake on his master's part that is responsible, or at least encourages it. For the master could have made sure that he was not put in charge in the first place, and that he was removed if he already held the post.

(6) But when estates are a long way away, so that the *paterfamilias* finds it difficult to visit them, then any kind of cultivation by free tenants is preferable to that of slave managers; particularly in the case of arable farming, since a tenant can do minimal damage to such a farm, unlike vineyards and orchards, while slaves can do a lot of damage. They may hire out the oxen and not pasture the other cattle properly and not do the ploughing properly, and claim that they have sown far more seed than they in fact have, and not look after what they have sown to make it grow properly, and lose a lot of the harvested grain during the threshing process through theft or carelessness. (7) They may steal it themselves or fail to take proper precautions against its theft by others or just not keep reliable accounts. The result is that neither the manager nor the slaves do their work properly and the value of the farm declines. That is why I think that an estate of this kind should be let to tenants if, as I said, the owner cannot be there himself.

Whatever the status of those who did the work, the *dominus*'s ultimate responsibility meant that a great deal of emphasis was put on the effectiveness of his supervision. Here again he was helped by the institution of slavery: it enabled an owner, through his slaves, to supervise estates and business operations at which he was physically unable to be present. A letter of Pliny's illustrates the conflict between two ideals: that a wealthy man of leisure finds managerial duties beneath him, and that the *bonus paterfamilias* effectively supervises his estates.

## 93  Pliny, *Letters* 9, 15

Gaius Plinius greets his friend Falco.

I had fled to my Tuscan estate in order to have the freedom to do as I pleased. But that is not possible even here: I am disturbed by vast numbers of petitions from the peasants all over the place, which I read with rather less pleasure than I am reading my own writings (and I am not reading those with any pleasure – (2) I am in the middle of revising some legal speeches, and it is cold and distasteful to do that after a lapse of time). The estate accounts are being so neglected that I might as well not be here. (3) However, I do occasionally get on my horse and act out the part of a *paterfamilias* to the extent of riding round some part of my property, but only for the exercise. Carry on with your custom of writing the news from Rome to us out in the country.

Ancient agricultural handbooks emphasise estate management (which was why they continued to be useful to landowners throughout the Middle Ages and later, even in countries with completely non-Mediterranean agricultural systems). There are special sections on the estate manager (*vilicus*), normally a slave.

## 94  Columella 1, 8

The next thing to think about is which slave to put in charge of which particular office and what jobs each should be given. My first advice is not to appoint as manager one of those slaves who are good-looking or who come from the ranks of those who perform specialised services in the city household. (2) This kind of slave is dedicated to sleep and idleness, and because he has been used to free time, athletics, race-meetings, the amphitheatre, dicing, wineshops and brothels, he spends all his time dreaming of this nonsense; and when that happens in farming, the owner loses not just the value of the slave, but of his entire property. You should select someone who has been inured to agricultural work from childhood and tested by experience. If you do not have anyone like this, you should put someone in charge who has already been used to hard work as a slave. (3) He should no longer be a young man, since this will detract from his authority to command, since old men do not like to obey a youngster; but he should not have reached old age yet either, or he will not have the stamina for work of the most strenuous kind. He should be middle aged and fit and know about agriculture, or at least be sufficiently dedicated to be able to learn quickly. There is no point in having one man in authority and someone else to tell him what work has to be done, (4) since a man who is just learning from one of those under him what ought to be done and how to go about doing it will not really be able to insist that it gets done. Even someone who cannot read and write can supervise an estate properly, so long as he has a first-rate memory. Cornelius Celsus[1] says that a manager of this sort brings his master money more often than he brings him his accounts – because he is illiterate, he cannot cook the figures so easily, and he would not dare to do so through a confederate who would know exactly what was going on. (5) To whomever is appointed manager, you must allocate a woman to live with him and keep him under control and also to help him in various things. The manager should also be warned against being on particularly good terms with any one of the slaves on the farm, let alone with anyone from outside. But occasionally he should confer a mark of distinction on any slave whom he sees working hard, and dedicated to the tasks assigned to him, by inviting him to dinner on a festival day. He must not make any religious sacrifices except if the master has told him to. (6) He must not let fortune-tellers or sorceresses on to the farm; both these types of silly superstition make unsophisticated people spend money, and lead to wrongdoing. He should not spend his time in town or at markets except to buy or sell something which is his business. (7) As Cato says, the manager should not go out a lot; he should not leave the boundaries of the estate except to find out about some agricultural technique, and even then he should only go to places from which he can get back (sc. on the same day). He must not allow any new tracks or paths to be made on the estate; and he should not receive anyone as a guest unless he is an *amicus* or close relative of his master.

(8) Those are the things he must be told to avoid; and he must be urged to make sure that twice as many metal tools and instruments are kept stored away in good condition as are required by the number of slaves, so that nothing will ever have

to be borrowed from one of the neighbours; for the expense in terms of the slave's labour being lost outweighs the cost of providing such extra equipment. (9) He should dress and clothe the slaves in a functional rather than an attractive way, so that they are protected against storms, frost and rain; long-sleeved coats, patchwork cloaks and hoods afford protection against all of these. If they have these, the weather will never be so bad that there is not some work they can do out in the open. (10) He should not merely be skilled at agricultural work; he should also have such personal qualities – in so far as this is possible in a slave – that he will exercise his authority neither irresponsibly nor brutally, and should always be giving encouragement to some of the better slaves, and should not be too hard on those who are less good, so that he will be feared for being severe rather than hated for being cruel. He will achieve this if he keeps watch over those under his authority so that they do nothing wrong, instead of finding that he has to punish delinquents as a result of his own incompetence.

*Note*

1  Celsus (reign of Tiberius) wrote an encyclopaedia on the skills a good Roman required, notably agriculture and medicine.

Although in classical Roman law slaves did not have the legal capacity to undertake the obligations of marriage, masters often allowed slave managers the privilege of a stable relationship with a female slave, the *vilica*, who also had important supervisory duties.

## 95  Columella 12, 3

(6)  In rainy weather and at times when the woman cannot do any agricultural work in the open because of cold or frost, she is to occupy herself with wool-work. To enable her to get on with the job of spinning and weaving and to make the others do it as well, wool should be prepared and ready-carded. It will do no harm if clothing for herself and the overseers and the other senior slaves is made at home in order to reduce the owner's expenses. (7) What she must always remember to do is to go round once the slaves have left the farmhouse and look for anyone who ought to

be out working in the fields; and if she finds any malingerer inside, who has escaped the notice of her husband, as does happen, she must ask him why he is not at work and find out whether he has stayed behind because he feels ill or because he is lazy. If she finds that the former is the case, she must immediately take him to the hospital, even if he is only pretending to be ill; for it is worthwhile to let someone who is exhausted by work take a day or two off and be looked after, rather than force him to work excessively so that he becomes really ill.

(8)   Finally, she ought to stay in one place as little as possible; her job is not to sit still, but sometimes to go to the loom, and teach the person working there any particular technique she knows, or to learn some such skill from someone who knows more than she does. Sometimes she should go to see those who are preparing the slaves' food. She must make sure that the kitchens, the cowsheds, and not least the pens, are properly cleaned. From time to time she should go and open up the sickroom, even if there are no patients there, and give it a clean so that it is in a proper and healthy state to receive anyone who may fall ill.

In the second century BC, Cato the Elder advised his slave farm manager (*vilicus*) on how to keep his wife, the *vilica*, under control. We may note his anxiety about unapproved religious activity. Many of the tasks mentioned continued to constitute a major part of the work done by women, even in the industrialised world, until recently.

## 96   Cato, *Agriculture* 143

Make sure that the *vilica* carries out her duties. If the master has given her to you as your wife, be satisfied with her. Make sure that she fears you. Do not let her be too extravagant. She should have as little as possible to do with neighbours or other women, and never invite them into the house with her. She must not accept invitations to meals or go out all the time. She must not offer sacrifices herself or ask someone else to do so on her behalf except on the master's or mistress's express orders. You should know that it is the master who sacrifices on behalf of all the servants (*familia*).

(2) She must be clean. She must keep the farm tidy and clean. She must see that the hearth is swept and tidy every night before going to bed. On the Kalends, Ides, Nones and other feast-days, she must put up a garland over the hearth. And on the same days she must offer supplication to the family *Lar* as well as she can. And she must ensure that she has food cooked for you and the other slaves.

(3) She should keep plenty of hens for eggs. She should keep dried pears, berries, figs, raisins, stewed berries and pears, grapes and quinces in jars, grapes and grape-pulp in underground containers; also fresh Praenestan nuts in underground containers. Every year she must carefully store jars of Scantian apples and other berries and fruit that are customarily kept as preserves. She must know how to grind good flour and clear spelt.

Inscriptions confirm that many *vilici* remained slaves despite their managerial responsibilities (see **165**; Wiedemann, GARS nos 152–4). The following inscription found near Monte Testaccio at Rome refers to the *domus* of the emperor. We may note differences in status between *procurator* and *vilicus*; only the procurator, a free (or freed-) man, could perform a legally recognised action such as granting land for a shrine. We may also note the subtle distinctions in status between the *vilici*, a *verna*, and the *plebs*.

## 97 ILS 3840 = CIL VI, 30983 (Rome)

Dedicated to the Divine Power of the Household of Augustus, to Aesculapius and to the Well-being (*Salus*) of Augustus by the association (of worshippers) of Well-being (*collegium salutar.*). The ground was assigned by the procurator of the patrimony of our (lord) Caesar; the building was constructed from the ground up by the overseers (*vilici*) of Galba's estates, Felix, house-born slave; Aspergus, bought from Regius (?); and Vindex, house-born slave (*verna*); and by the (?) free workers (*plebs imm.*) Actalius Januarius, Ulpius Sextianus, Cluturius Secundus . . . (and fifty-three others).

The Benedictine rule gives details of the daily routine on a productive estate (including the fact that necessities of nature were to be seen to before daybreak (Lauds, morning prayers): paragraph 8).

## 98 *Rule of St Benedict*, chs 39–41

(39) We think it sufficient for the daily meals, both those taken at the sixth and ninth hours, to have always two cooked dishes,[1] to allow for different monks' inabilities (sc. to chew). Thus if someone is unable to eat from one dish, he may sustain himself from the other. So two cooked dishes should be enough for all the brothers; but if fruit or fresh vegetables can be provided, these may be added as a third dish. One pound by weight of bread per day should be enough, whether there is one meal or both lunch and an evening meal. When there is an evening meal, a third of the pound is to be kept back by the cellarer and given to the monks then. [The abbot may increase the allowance for monks doing hard work.] . . . And the same shall not be given to young children, but a lesser amount, and economy should be exercised with regard to all. . . . The meat of four-footed animals should not be consumed by anyone, except for those who are very weak and the sick.

(40) Recognising the weakness of human nature, we think that one hemina[2] of wine is to be enough per person per day, but geographical conditions, hard work, or the summer heat may require more; the decision should rest with the prior.

Chapter 41 lists the times at which meals are to be taken.

Easter to Whitsun: the midday meal at the sixth hour, the evening meal at nightfall.

From Whitsun on through the whole of the summer: unless the monks have agricultural work to do or there is a heatwave, there is to be fasting up to the ninth hour on Wednesday and Friday, and on the other days a midday meal at the sixth hour. . . .

From the Ides of September until the beginning of Lent: the main meal is to be at the ninth hour.

During Lent, up until Easter: the main meal is to be in the

evening. The evening meal itself is to be arranged so that the diners will not need the light of lamps. Everything must be eaten by the light of day.

*Notes*

1  *Pulmentaria*: 'relish' as opposed to carbohydrates.
2  *Hemina*: half a sextarius, or 0.273 litres.

Chapter 48 prescribes the daily routine. From Easter to the 1st October there is to be manual work from the first to the fourth hour; reading during the fifth and sixth hours; lunch; then an afternoon nap (or silent reading); prayer at the middle of the eighth hour; then more work. From October until the start of Lent, the rule prescribes reading during the first and second hour; work from the third until the ninth hour; and more reading after supper. The daily routine for Lent (the forty days before Easter) consists of reading from dawn until the third hour, followed by work until the tenth hour. Sundays are reserved entirely for reading.

Chapter 55 describes the monks' allocation of clothing. Allowances are to be made for different climatic conditions, but in principle they are to have one *cuculla* (outer gown) and tunic each for summer, and one for winter, and a scapular (cloak going over the shoulders) for working, plus shoes and leggings. If they go on a journey, they are to be issued with *femoralia* (underpants). In accordance with ancient economic theory, Benedict specifies that all clothing should be obtained locally, and as cheaply as possible.

# V

# THE LIFE-CYCLE

## Mortality and old age

It is not easy to reconstruct averages for life expectancy or population pyramids for antiquity. The following passage illustrates a number of reasons for this:

(1) the unreliability of figures recorded in manuscripts: many of those Pliny gives are not written in words but numbers, and about 5 per cent of the figures in any handwritten list tend to be copied incorrectly.

(2) Although Augustus instituted provision for the registration of (legitimate citizen) births, unawareness of exact age (both one's own and that of one's close relatives) seems to have been fairly common in the Roman world. In private contexts, such as gravestones recording age of death, multiples of five are noticeably over-represented. A similar rounding-up effect probably occurred also in census declarations. Precision is found, in contrast, where there was an active official interest in securing it (as, e.g., in official tax documents from Egypt). Presumably also the wealthier, office-holding families would take care to ensure that their relevant personal information was on record. For most people, however, occasions would seldom arise when establishing exact age served any practical purpose.

(3) Where extreme old age warrants respect, the oldest members of the community may claim to be older (sometimes much older) than they actually are. The number of people claiming to be centenarians in Vespasian's census of 72–4 AD was proportionately something like twenty to fifty times higher than that reported in the Chinese census of 1981 (see Wiedemann, ACRE, p. 43 n. 15). It is unlikely that the remarkably high figures given on some tombstones are always reliable (e.g., ILS 1680 from Carthage, referring to Victor, slave of Augustus, and his wife Urbica, said to have died aged 102 and 80 respectively).

(4) Ancient writers do not select anecdotes for being typical, but exceptional; and they find exaggerated claims more interesting than what Pliny here calls 'agreed facts'.

## 99  Pliny, *Natural History* 7, 48/156-8, 162-4

Let us discuss facts that are agreed: it is almost certain that the reign of King Arganthonius at Cadiz lasted for eighty years, and they think that it began in his fortieth year. There is no doubt that Masinissa ruled for sixty, and that Gorgias the Sicilian lived to 108. Quintus Fabius Maximus was an augur for 63. Marcus Perperna, and more recently Lucius Volusius Saturninus, outlived all those whom they had asked to give their opinions when they had been consuls. Perperna left behind only eight of the senators he had selected during his censorship, and lived to his ninety-eighth year. In this connection, it also occurs to me to mention that there was only one five-year period in which no single senator died; that was following the census of Flaccus and Albinus, in the year 579 from the foundation of the city (175 BC). Marcus Valerius Corvinus lived for a hundred years; 46 years separated his first from his sixth consulship. No one else equalled his record of holding curule office twenty-one times, but the pontifex Metellus lived for as many years.

Among women, Rutulus's [wife] Livia died at 97, Statilia, a lady from a noble household in the time of Claudius, at 99, Cicero's [wife] Terentia at 103, Ofilius's [wife] Clodia at 115; and she bore fifteen children. The actress Lucceia declaimed on stage at the age of 100. The *chanteuse* Galeria Copiola was brought back on to the stage in AD 9 at the votive games held for the recovery of Augustus, when she was 104; she had been brought on to the stage for the first time ninety-one years before by the plebeian aedile Marcus Pomponius in 82 BC, and as an old woman had been brought on again by Pompey the Great to give a special performance at the dedication of his great theatre. . . .

After more information about the longevity of actors, Pliny continues:

(162)  We also have the empirical evidence of the most recent

census which the Emperors Caesar Vespasian, father and son, held three years ago during their censorship. We do not have to give all the details, but give some examples from the region in between the Apennines and the river Po. At Parma three people declared that they were 120, at Brixellum one; at Parma two declared 125, at Placentia one 130 and at Faventia one female; at Bononia Lucius Terentius, son of Marcus, declared 135, and at Rimini Marcus Aponius even declared 140 and Tertulla 137. In the hills to the south of Placentia is the town of Veleia; here six persons registered at 110, four at 120 and one at 150 (Marcus Mucius Felix, son of Marcus, of the Galerian tribe). In order not to waste more time on matters that are established as true, in the eighth region of Italy fifty-four persons aged over a hundred were registered, plus fourteen of 110, two of 125, four of 130, as many of 135 or 137, and three of 140.

An alternative way of estimating the number of years a Roman might have expected to live has been to use an excerpt from a handbook for Roman tax officials with a formula for calculating the number of years a person was expected to survive at a particular age. Tax officials needed to know the value of maintenance grants (*alimenta*) which testators sometimes left in their wills (though we may note that the jurist Aemilius Macer admits that the formula that actually tended to be used was very much cruder than that prescribed by Ulpian). We may note that Ulpian did not distinguish between males and females, and that no allowance needed to be made for high mortality among children. Nevertheless there is enough cumulative evidence to support the view that life expectancy at birth lay around 21 years; that a third of children died before they were 1; that less than half survived to age 5; that 40 per cent might expect to see their twentieth birthday; and that one in ten might reach the age of 60. Over a third of the population may have been under 15, and under 5 per cent over 60. (See bibliography: Life-expectancy.)

## 100  *Digest* 35, 2.68.pr. (from Aemilius Macer, *On the Five-Per-Cent Tax,* book 2)

Ulpian writes that the following formula is to be applied when calculating the value of maintenance provisions:

'For a person aged between birth and 20, thirty years' maintenance should be estimated (and the Falcidian Law applies to this amount);

for a person aged between 20 and 25, the estimate is twenty-eight years;

from 25 to 30, twenty-five years.

from 30 to 35, twenty-two years.

from 35 to 40, twenty years.

from 40 to 50, as many years as are left for the person to reach the age of 60, less one year.

from 50 to 55, nine years;

from 55 to 60, seven years;

over 60 (whatever the age someone is), five years.'

Ulpian says that this is the formula we should properly use also in calculating the value of (a legacy of) income. In practice however we estimate

(a) thirty years for anyone aged between between birth and 30, and

(b) for anyone over 30 as many years as are left before he reaches 60. Thirty years is thus the maximum estimate.

Consequently when a legacy of income is left to a city or community, either without specific conditions or to pay for games, it is calculated as worth thirty years' income.


There is some evidence of mechanisms for the relief of the old and the sick at the level of the community – as had been organised to some extent in fifth-century BC Athens, and by late antiquity were being developed by Christian churches. *Digest* 30, 122 refers to bequests made to cities 'for the maintenance of those of infirm age, that is the old, or boys and girls'. From the end of the first century AD on, many cities in Italy organised 'alimentary schemes' which consisted of grants to poor families to help them bring up additional children, especially boys who might later serve in the legions.

But in general it was the *paterfamilias* (and, where he could not, the friends of the household) who had the responsibility to ensure that the old and sick as well as the young were fed and clothed. Classical literature frequently couples the very old and the very young (together with women) as needing particular protection. In the sixth century AD, St Benedict prescribed:

**101**   *Rule of St Benedict*, **chs 36–7**

The abbot should be very careful that (the sick) suffer no neglect. Any sick brothers should be allocated separate accommodation and someone God-fearing, hard-working and caring to look after them. The sick should have the opportunity to take a bath as often as necessary, though this privilege should be allowed more sparingly to those who are healthy, especially the younger ones. The eating of meat should also be permitted to those who are sick and weak, to help them to recuperate. But when they have got well again, they should all give up meat in accordance with general practice. The abbot must be particularly careful that the sick do not suffer neglect at the hands of the cellarers or servants; for it is his responsibility if anything fails to be done properly by any of his disciples.

Although human nature itself makes us be considerate to the two age groups of the old and of children, nevertheless the authority of this Rule should also make provision for them. Their weakness should always be taken into account, and the full rigour of the Rule as regards food should in no respect be adhered to. Compassionate consideration should be given them, and they should be allowed to anticipate the regular hours.

As in many agrarian societies, there was much emphasis on respecting the old; but that respect tended to be seen as an ideal ascribed to a past golden age. Valerius Maximus lists it among 'ancient customs'.

**102   Valerius Maximus, 2, 1.9**

Youth used to award old age total and deliberate respect, just as if older men were the common parents of the young. Thus on a day when the Senate was meeting, young men would accompany one of the senators who was either a relative or a friend of their father's and remain standing at the doors waiting for him until they performed the same office by accompanying him home. By choosing to wait in this way they strengthened both their bodies and their minds for the active sustaining of public duties, and by respectfully exerting themselves in this way, they themselves taught themselves those virtues that would soon become publicly known. When they were invited to a dinner-party they used to take pains to ask who else would be present at the dinner in order to avoid taking their places before any older man arrived, and when the table had been removed they allowed (their elders) to get up and leave first. It is clear from this how sparingly and quietly they would speak in the presence of their elders, even at mealtimes.

The Roman emphasis on the rights of the *paterfamilias* ensured that old men could continue to control their property until they died, and if the wealth produced by that property was sufficient, enjoy a reasonable material existence.

## 103  Pliny, *Letters* 3, 1

Gaius Plinius greets his friend Calvisius Rufus.

I do not know if I have ever had a more pleasant time than that which I recently spent with Spurinna – so much so that there is no one I would prefer to be like in old age (supposing that I were allowed to reach old age); for nothing can be better-arranged than his daily routine. (2) It gives me pleasure when a man's life-style is as well regulated as the fixed passage of the stars. That applies to the old in particular; for there is nothing unbecoming in young men leading a life that is somewhat turbulent and disorganised, but for the old everything ought to be peaceful and orderly, since it is unseemly to be ambitious at the end of one's working life. (3) Spurinna unfailingly accepts this rule, and he has a set order, as it were, and routine for the performance even of insignificant things (at least, they would be insignificant if they were not done every day). (4) He stays in bed in the morning, asks for his shoes at the second hour, takes a walk for three miles, and exercises his mind as much as his body. If friends are with him, he discusses matters of serious interest; if not, he is read to – sometimes he is read to when friends are present, if they do not mind. (5) Then he seats himself, and the reading or (preferably) conversation continues. Later he gets into his carriage together with his wife (a wonderful lady) or one of his friends – recently it was me. . . .

(8) When the time for his bath is announced (at the ninth hour in winter, and at the eighth in summer), he will walk in the sun without his clothes, if there is no breeze. Then he plays ball energetically and for quite a long time; this is another of the exercises with which he struggles against old age. After the bath he sits down, but puts his meal off for some time; in the meantime he listens to a reading of something light and agreeable. . . . (10) This is how he has passed his seventy-seventh year with his sight and hearing as good as ever, his body vigorous and supple, and old age having brought him nothing but good sense. (11) I pray for and look forward to such a life-style, which I intend to enter upon just as soon as my own age allows the trumpet to sound the retreat.

For ordinary small farmers, the best insurance against incapacity in old age was to raise children who would look after them; the Roman emphasis on *patria potestas* gave them security. For elderly peasants with no children to look after them, only reserves of cash would tide them over a long illness or a period of scarcity such as accompanied the civil wars of the first century BC.

## 104  *Digest* 32, 79.1 (Celsus)

Suppose a legacy is made using these words: 'I give and bestow any of my furniture which will be in such and such a place . . .'. Proculus says that if any money is kept in that place to be used for lending at interest, it is not meant to be included in the legacy; but money that is kept there as an insurance (as people used to do during the period of the civil wars) is included. He had heard elderly peasants (*rusticos senes*) say that money was frittered away if it was not kept as a nest-egg (*peculium*); by 'nest-egg' they meant what they had put aside as an insurance.

It has been argued that for those who did not control wealth, the reality of old age was very different. Nevertheless legacies to old dependants are mentioned in wills (such as that of 'Dasumius', **158**, p. 136), and the *Digest* has several references to men making provision for maintenance payments (*alimenta*) in their wills: hence the need for Ulpian's Life Table (**100**, pp. 88f.). The concern shown in some wills to preserve the standard of living of freedmen shows how much they were thought to be 'part of the family'.

## 105   *Digest* 33, 2.33 (Scaevola)

Suppose a will says, 'I wish to give Sempronius those things that I provided him with while I was alive'. This man was living in the testator's house, which was granted to one of the heirs as a legacy. The question was raised, Did the heir have an obligation to house the man? Scaevola answered that there was no reason why he should not have this obligation.

(1) A will contained these words: 'I wish to provide those of my freedmen to whom I do not specifically leave anything with those things that I provided them with while I was alive.' The question was raised, Was there an obligation to house those freedmen who were living in their patron's house on the day of his death? He replied that there appeared to be such an obligation.

(2) A woman wrote as follows in a codicil: 'I request you to allow my old and infirm freedmen Negidius, Titius and Dio, to grow old in the places they now frequent.' The question was raised, Did this sentence imply that the freedmen mentioned had a right in trust (*fideicommissum*) to the income of the estates on which they lived, given that there was no doubt that they had a right to the other things which were specifically left to each of them? He replied that the words as stated requested the following: that the heirs should allow them to live there in the same style as she herself had allowed.

A famous literary example of such provision is the case of Pliny's old nurse.

## 106   Pliny, *Letters* 6, 3

Thank you for arranging the management of the little farm which I had presented to my old nurse. It was worth 100,000 sesterces when I originally gave it to her; afterwards the income decreased and the value of the estate fell accordingly. With you in charge, it will recover its former value. You must remember that it is not just trees and soil with which you have been entrusted (although that too), but rather with the gift that I have made; and that it is as important to me who gave it as to her who received it, that it should be as profitable as possible.

One way of ensuring that those who had little or no property of their own would have an acceptable old age was by giving them jobs as temple-keepers.

### 107 ILS 4999 = CIL VI, 2210 (Rome)

To the Propitious Gods
Claudia Quinta, daughter of Tiberius, for Gaius Julius Hymetus, temple-keeper of Diana Planciana, her child-minder [in Greek] and her guide, who was also her legal guardian when she was orphaned; because he rendered her his service as tutor with absolute honesty;
and for his brother Gaius Julius Epitynchanus, and for Julia Sporis, the daughter of her nurse, and for her freedmen and freedwomen and their descendants.

We may note that the *Digest* implies that most old people had lost their teeth — for if keeping one's teeth were a criterion for good health, then 'no old man would be considered sound' (21, 11). For a slave to have lived an active life into his sixties as caretaker of an imperial villa at Formii was considered worthy of note by his freedman son.

### 108 ILS 1583 = CIL X, 6093 (Caieta)

To Laeones,
home-born slave, steward, who lived 66 years and spent his time to the last day of his life in looking after the (imperial) residence with the greatest care: Amazonicus, freedman of the Augusti,

procurator, with his brothers dedicated this to his dearest father, who well deserved it.

Old slaves would continue to be maintained so long as they were useful for something: as child-minders (cf. **128**, p. 108) or door-keepers (**87**, p. 74). But a thrifty householder like Cato the Elder advocated selling off old and sick slaves, despite the moral disapproval this encountered (Wiedemann, GARS, 201; cf. GARS, 203; Martial, *Epigrams* 11, 70). Seneca's remarks about the keeper of a country villa are in crass contrast to Valerius Maximus's respect for old age, and rather betray a callous attitude to an old age unprotected by wealth.

## 109 Seneca, *Letters* 12

Wherever I turn, I see evidence of my increasing senility. I was visiting an estate of mine outside Rome and complaining about the expense of repairing the dilapidated building. My manager assured me that that was not the result of neglect on his part: he was doing what he could, but the fact was that the building was old. Actually, the house was built under my own supervision – what is to happen to me, if stones of the same age as myself are in such a crumbling state? (2) I was upset at what he had said, and took advantage of the next suitable occasion to show my temper. 'These plane-trees are obviously not being looked after' I said; 'There are no leaves on them, the branches are all knotted and parched, and the bark is flaking off those squalid trunks. That would not happen if someone was digging round them and watering them properly.' He swore by my own spirit (*genius*) that he was doing all he could, that there was no respect in which his efforts were falling short – the fact was that the trees were old. Between ourselves, I planted them myself, I saw them put out their first growth of leaves. (3) I walked up to the entrance. 'Who, I said, is that decrepit fellow? How appropriate that he should have been posted at the door – he's about to take leave of us. Where on earth did you get hold of him? What possessed you to steal a corpse from someone else?' But the fellow said to me, 'Don't you recognise me? I'm Felicio – you used to give me puppets at the Saturnalia. I'm the son of your manager Philositus.

I was your playmate when we were little.' 'The man's completely mad,' I said. 'Now he's turned into a little boy and playmate of mine. Could be true though – he's toothless as a child.'

## Fertility

The desire for children of one's own as a support in old age conflicted with the wish to leave one's property to the persons of one's choice – which, especially for the very rich, could mean 'buying' support and friendship in old age from so-called legacy-hunters (see **153**, p. 127). In both the republican and the imperial period, Roman leaders, concerned about the manpower requirements of the Roman army, felt that more children should be brought up. When Augustus passed legislation to give couples additional incentives to have several children, he is reported to have made the following speech to those members of the equestrian order who were bringing up children.

### 110 Cassius Dio, 56.3

Even though you are only a few in comparison with the entire population of the city, and you are far fewer than those others who are not willing to undertake their responsibilities, for this very reason I praise you all the more and wish to thank you heartily, because you are obedient and are helping in re-populating your community. For Rome will be populous in future as a result of the way you are living your lives now. At the beginning there were few of us, but then we married and raised children and came to be not only better but also more numerous than other peoples. We must remember this, and make up for the mortality of our human nature by means of the unending succession of future generations, like so many torch-bearers, so that through one another we may make immortal the single respect in which we fall short of divine happiness. It was for this purpose above all that that first and greatest of gods who fashioned us divided the human race into two, male and female, and implanted into us sexual passion and the need for intercourse, and made that intercourse fruitful; so that even mortality might become in a way immortal by the birth of new generations. Even the gods are thought of as male and female, and it is said that some have fathered others, and some have been born of others. So marriage and the raising of children have been thought good even by those beings who have no need of such things.

Therefore you have done right in imitating the gods and emulating your fathers in bringing children into the world in the same way as they brought you into the world, and so that future generations may respect you and refer to you as their ancestors just as you think of them and call them your ancestors, and so that you may hand down to others the great and glorious achievements that have been left to you, and so that you yourselves may leave to others whom you have begotten the wealth which your ancestors created and left to you. What can be better than a wife who exercises personal self-control, stays at home, can manage the house for you and bring up your children; give you joy when you are well, and comfort when you are sick; share your successes and console you for your failures; hold back the reckless excesses of your youth, and dilute the harsh austerity of your old age. How can it be anything but a pleasure to raise up from the ground a child who has been born from the two of you and to feed and educate it, a physical and mental mirror of yourself, so that, as it grows up, another self is created? Is it anything but the greatest blessing to leave behind as our successor when we leave this life an heir both to our family and to our property; one who is our own, born of our own essence, so that only the mortal part of us passes away, while we live on in the child who succeeds us, so that you will not fall into the hands of strangers and suffer an extinction as total as in warfare?

The thoughts on procreation as Dio relates them are commonplaces of Greek philosophy (see, for instance, Plato's *Symposium*), but Augustus's ideas appear elsewhere in characteristically Roman terms.

## 111 Juvenal, *Satire* 13, 70–2

It is good that you have given the country and the Roman people a citizen, if you make sure that he is suitable material for the country, useful in the fields, useful in all the activities of war and peace.

Many scholars believe that abortion, infanticide and exposition were widely practised in the Roman world as ways of limiting the number of children (and in particular daughters) a family had to support. (See bibliography: Infanticide, abortion and birth control; some of the evidence is translated in R. K. Sherk, *The Roman Empire: Augustus to Hadrian* (Cambridge, 1988), no. 188.) Many of the literary references to exposed or supposititious infants are associated with mythological or folk-tale motifs. Ovid tells the story of the girl Iphis, whose mother Telethusa brought her up as a boy to avoid exposure at birth. In the end the goddess Isis turns her into a boy to allow her (now him) to marry Ianthe.

## 112   Ovid, *Metamorphoses* 9, 669–81

Although Ligdus was of free birth, his family was poor. Nevertheless he was a man of honour and integrity. When his pregnant wife was near giving birth, he said to her: 'There are two things that I wish: that your labour may be easy, and that your child will be a boy. A daughter is too expensive, and we do not have the resources. With great regret I have to say that if it should be a girl, we will have to let her die.' When he finished, tears washed both the face of the man who gave the order, and the woman to whom it was given.

Exact statistics for how many children Roman women were likely to have during their child-bearing years are hard to come by. As with mortality, the evidence is primarily anecdotal.

## 113   Pliny, *Natural History* 7, 13/57, 59–60

Some women produce only either female or male children; but generally they alternate, as with the twelve children the mother of the Gracchi bore, or the nine born by Germanicus's wife Agrippina. . . . Quintus Metellus Macedonicus left six children and eleven grandchildren; but including daughters-in-law and sons-in-law and all those who owed him the title 'father' (i.e., whose *paterfamilias* he was), twenty-seven. In the official record of Augustus's reign can be found the statement that on 9 April 5 BC, Gaius Crispinus Hilarus, an ordinary citizen of Fiesole, went in procession to the Capitol to sacrifice, preceded by his eight children (two of them daughters), his twenty-seven grandchildren and eighteen great-grandchildren by his sons, and the eight wives of his grandsons.

Only three of Gracchus's twelve children survived into adulthood, and only six of Agrippina's. A small number of inscriptions confirm the impression that fewer than half the babies born alive had an expectation of living to adulthood. In other words, every Roman couple needed to have five children if the population was to reproduce itself.

## 114   CIL III, 3572 (Aquincum/Budapest)

Here I lie, Veturia by name and descent, a married woman. I was Fortunatus's wife, my father was Veturius. Sadly, I lived for just thrice nine years, and was married for twice eight. I slept with one man, I was married to one man. I died after having borne six children; one of them survives me. Titus Julius Fortunatus, centurion of the Second Auxiliary legion, set this up to his incomparable and exceptionally respectful wife.

Many inscriptions refer to the grief of parents whose children died young. One example:

## 115   ILS 1660 = CIL VI, 8517 (Rome)

To the Spirits of the Deceased Philete.
Epitynchanus, treasurer of Hesychius, overseer of the military exchequer, to his sweetest daughter, who lived for six years and died on her birthday as she entered upon her seventh year.

dis man. Philete Epitynchanus Hesychi dispensatoris fisci castrensis arcarius filiae dulcissimae, quae vixit ann.VI, obit natali suo, intrans annum septimum.

The shortcomings of medical knowledge in antiquity made child-birth far more dangerous than it is today. This was especially the case for girls who married and might have several children while still in their teens, like Herennia Cervilla, who died aged 18 years and 30 days, leaving three children (AE 1985, no. 355; Villa Potenza, near Ricina). An inscription from Ancyra/Ankara refers to the wife of a member of the staff of a man who had been consul in AD 166.

## 116   ILS 1914 = CIL III, 6759

To the Spirits of the Deceased Aeturnia Zotica.
Annius Flavianus, one of the ten lictors of Fufidius Pollio, governor of Galatia, to his well-deserving wife. She lived for 15 years, 5 months and 18 days; she died sixteen days after giving birth to her first child, leaving a son alive.

d.m. Aeturniae Zotice. Annius Flavianus Dec[urialis] lictor Fufid. Pollionis Leg. Gal. Coniugi b.m. vixit ann. XV mens. V dieb. XVIII quae partu primo post diem XVI relicto filio decessit.

A young wife's ignorance and inexperience during her first pregnancy might have disastrous consequences for herself or for the child. Pliny's Calpurnia (see **70**, p. 62) is a well-known instance. His letters to her grandfather and her aunt are revealing in their assumptions about what would be the primary concern of either – for the man, an heir, for the woman, the niece's health.

## 117   Pliny, *Letters* 8, 10 and 11

Gaius Pliny greets his grandfather-in-law, Fabatus.
Just as it is your dearest wish for us to present you with a great-grandchild, so you will be particularly disappointed to hear that your granddaughter has had a miscarriage; she was unaware that she was pregnant, as so often happens with young girls (*puellariter*), and consequently failed to be as careful as expectant mothers should be, and continued to do various things that should have been given up. She has suffered for her mistakes by what she has gone through, to the extent of almost losing her life. (2) So you must both responsibly come to terms with the fact that your old age has been disappointed of a descendant who was already on

the way, and also give thanks to the gods that while they have withheld great-grandchildren for the time being, they have at least preserved your granddaughter. That they will present you with great-grandchildren is a certain hope, proved by the fact that your granddaughter conceived, though the occasion turned out to be so unhappy. (3) I am consoling, advising and supporting you with the same arguments as I apply to myself. For you long for great-grandchildren no more ardently than I for children; as my descendants and yours, they will have easy access to public office, they will be widely known, and I will be able to leave them a well-established ancestry (*non subitas imagines*). May they be born, and turn our present sadness to joy. Keep well.

Gaius Plinius to his dear Hispulla.

When I think of the way your feelings towards your brother's daughter are more tender than a mother's love, it occurs to me that I should give you the news that ought to be left till the end first, so that joy will leave no room for worry. But then your relief might turn to fear, and you would rejoice at her escape from danger only to be shocked by the seriousness of the danger. (2) She is happy again now, restored to herself and to me and beginning to recuperate; as she gets better she can assess the crisis she has passed through. For it was a serious crisis (there is no harm in saying that now), for which she is not to blame, though her youth may be. Hence the miscarriage, and the tragic proof of an undetected pregnancy. (3) Hence also you may be certain that, although your wish to be consoled for your deceased brother by a grandson or granddaughter of his has not yet been granted, that wish has been deferred rather than denied, since she whom you hope to bear that child is well. I would also like you to explain what has happened to your father, since women are more sympathetic about such things (*paratior apud feminas venia*).

## Upbringing and education

The ideal of the household as autonomous implied that it should not just produce its own labour force in the form of free and slave children, but also see that these children were properly trained for adult life (cf. 7, p. 10). In contrast to Greece, education remained primarily the responsibility of the individual household.

### 118 Plutarch, *Cato the Elder* 20, 4–7

When his son was born, Cato thought that only state affairs were important enough to prevent him from attending whenever his wife bathed the baby and put on his nappies. She herself nursed him with her own milk. . . .

When the child was capable of learning, Cato himself took responsibility and taught him letters – although he had a specialist slave called Chilon who was himself a teacher who had many pupils of his own. Cato himself says that he did not think it right for his son to be disciplined by a slave, to have his ears pulled by a slave for being tardy at his lessons, or to owe such a valuable asset as education to a slave. Cato himself taught him letters, taught him the laws and taught him athletics. He instructed him in how to throw a spear, fight in armour, to ride on horseback and to box; he also taught him to endure heat and cold, and to swim through whirlpools and river-rapids. He says that he wrote the book entitled the 'Histories' in his own hand and in large letters to enable his son to learn about the laws and customs of Rome at home. And he was as careful to avoid saying anything inappropriate in his son's presence as in that of a vestal virgin.

After his seizure of supreme power, Augustus tried to represent himself as an exemplary Roman father.

### 119 Suetonius, *Augustus* 64

He had three grandsons by Agrippa and Julia, Gaius, Lucius and Agrippa; and two granddaughters, Julia and Agrippina. He gave Julia in marriage to Lucius Paullus, the son of the censor, and Agrippina to his wife's grandson Germanicus. He adopted Gaius and Lucius into his own household, having 'bought' them from their father Agrippa by the procedure of 'Coin and Scales' (*per assem et libras emptos*),[1] and when they were still young he gave them political responsibility and sent them out to command provinces and armies when they were consuls-designate.

His daughter and granddaughters he brought up in such a way that he even got them used to spinning and banned them from saying or doing anything that could not be done in public and be put down in the daily records; and he prevented them from having any contacts with outsiders to such a degree that he once wrote to Lucius Vinicius, a well-known and good-looking young man, telling him that he had behaved outrageously in coming to greet his daughter at Baiae. He taught his grandsons letters and swimming and other basic skills mostly himself, and took particular pains to get them to copy his own handwriting. Whenever they ate with him, they had to sit on the lowest couch, and when he went on a journey they either had to walk in front of his carriage or ride at his side.

*Note*

1 This is a reference to the procedures accompanying adoption.

In late antiquity, too, a high-ranking senator was never too busy to concern himself with his son's education.

### 120 Symmachus, *Letters* 3, 20

Now that my son is beginning to learn Greek, I have been accompanying him in his studies for a second time, as though I were the same age. For the obligation to ensure that our children find pleasure in literature as well as labour, bids us to become children again.

This did not prevent wealthy parents from delegating the less pleasant or more time-consuming aspects of child-rearing to others. One of the most important figures in the life of a young Roman of wealthy family – or one whose mother had to return to work immediately because of poverty or because she was a skilled slave – was the wet-nurse (cf. **106**, pp. 93f., or the *mammula* celebrated in ILS 8532). Contracts for hiring wet-nurses appear in the *Digest* (50, 13.1.14; 24, 1.28.1 – minding the children of slave-girls, *ancillae*). It was thought that children drank in something of the character of their nurses with their milk, and there was much discussion of the morality of having children brought up by nurses instead of by their own mothers (e.g., Soranus 1, 19–21).

### 121 Aulus Gellius, 12, 1

Once when I was listening to the philosopher Favorinus it was announced that the wife of one of his disciples had shortly before given birth, and that he had been granted the gift of a son. 'Let us go to visit the child'[1] he said, 'and to offer the father our congratulations.' It was a senatorial family of high status. All of us who were there at the time went along together and followed Favorinus to the house he was going to, and entered along with him. He embraced the man and congratulated him, and sat down in the front part of the house. When he had finished asking how long the labour had lasted, and how difficult the birth had been, and heard that the girl was having a rest, exhausted by the effort and long period without sleep, he started to chat at greater length and said,

'I don't doubt that she will be breast-feeding the child with her own milk.'

When the girl's mother told him that she ought to be spared, and that nurses had to be found for the boy, so that the difficult and burdensome business of nursing should not be added to the pains of child-birth, he said, 'I beg you, woman, let her be a complete mother of her own son in every respect. What kind of unnatural, incomplete and half-category of mother is it, to have given birth and then immediately to cast the child away? To feed in your own womb something you do not know and have never seen, but then not to feed with your own milk a living human being whom you see, who is crying for his mother's help! Are you one of those who think that nature gave women their nipples to be like large-size beauty spots decorating their breasts rather than in order to feed their children?'

*Note*

1 Reading *puerum*. The alternative reading is *puerperam*, 'the new mother'.

For a well-to-do mother to have fed her babies herself was considered worthy of note.

## 122   ILS 8451 = CIL VI, 19128 (Rome)

To Gratia Alexandria,
an outstanding exemplar of modesty. She even brought up her
children with the milk of her own breasts. Her husband Pudens,
imperial freedman, (set this up) to a woman who deserved it. She
lived for 24 years, 3 months and 16 days.

Older children might be left in the care of a male slave child-minder, the
*paedagogus*, often too old or sick to do any productive work. Such slaves
often remained deeply loyal to their erstwhile charges, as in the case of
Livia Medullina, who died on the day when the later Emperor Claudius
was to have married her.

## 123   ILS 199 = CIL X, 6561 (Velitrae)

To Medullina, daughter of Camillus,
espoused to Tiberius Claudius Nero Germanicus.
The freedman Acratus, her *paedagogus*.

Young children of pre-school age were considered a delight or 'pet'
(*deliciae*) for those who could afford them. Slave *alumni* might be freed
before their deaths, even if very young (some of these might have been
the natural children of their patrons); e.g., AE 1983, no. 253 (Carignano,
S. Italy): 'To Seppius, sweetest *alumnus*, who lived 4 years 5 months. His
patron Seppius Proculus had this made: he well deserved it.' Martial
celebrated several such *deliciae*:

## 124   Martial, *Epigrams* 6, 28 and 29

Glaucia, Melior's well-known freedman, lies buried beneath this
slab of marble in a tomb by the Flaminian Way; he died to the
grief of all Rome, the short-lived delight of his loving patron. His
habits were chaste, his modesty unblemished, his intellect sharp,
his beauty fortunate. The boy had scarcely added one year to
twice six harvests. You who mourn as you pass by, may you have
nothing to mourn for.

Glaucia was not an ordinary household slave nor a child of the profit-making slave-market, but a boy worthy of his master's sacred love; at an age when he could not yet appreciate a patron's gifts, he was already Melior's freedman. He had been granted both good manners and beauty; who was sweeter than him? And what was more beautiful than his Apollo-like smile? Life is short for excessive good fortune, and old age rare. Whatever it is that you love, pray that it does not give too much pleasure.

## 125 Martial, *Epigrams* 5, 34 and 10, 61

My father Fronto, Flaccilla my mother, with a kiss I commend little Erotion to you, my delight; let her have no fear of the black shades and the frightful jaws of the hound of Tartarus. She would have entered the frosts of her sixth winter, had she not died as many days before [her sixth birthday]. Let her play her pranks on you as her old patrons, and chatter my name with her stammering mouth. May the turf lie lightly on her and may you, earth, not be a heavy weight upon her; for she was no great weight on you.

Here rests Erotion, her shade slipped away, whom her sixth winter called away at the summons of Fate. Whoever you may be who owns this little farm after me, grant the annual sacrifice to her tiny soul; if you do that, then may this tombstone on your land be the only thing you have to mourn, may your *Lar* last for ever, may your household (*turba*) be well.

That the word *deliciae* need have no pederastic connotation is shown by the fact that parents might describe their own children as such.

## 126 ILS 1570 = CIL VI, 8514 (Rome)

To the Spirits of the Deceased.
To Primigenius, pet of Epagathus, freedman of Augustus and procurator of the army treasury; Ephebus made this for his son.

**127   ILS 8470 = CIL VI, 5163 (Rome)**

Manius Allienus Romanus, illegitimate, died aged 22.
The girl Gutta, his pet, died on the same day, cremated on the
same pyre, aged 7.
Manius Allienus Antiochus, freedman of Manius;
Alliena Daphnis, his freedwoman (?); cremated together.
Manius Allienus Romanus of the tribe Cluentia, illegitimate, died
aged 11.

Future emperors were hardly typical of the Roman population; and
biographical accounts stress their miraculous and semi-divine nature even
as infants. But some typical elements emerge: a new-born baby was
placed on the ground for his *pater* to acknowledge him by lifting him up;
the baby was named on the day of purification (*dies lustricus*: the eighth
for girls, the ninth for boys); high mortality rates meant that one of the
parents often died while the child was still young; and the *paedagogus*
might be as important as the parents in the child's upbringing.

**128   Suetonius, *Nero* 6**

Nero was born at Antium, just nine months after the death of
Tiberius, on 15 December, exactly as the sun was rising, so that
he was touched by the sun's rays almost before being placed on
the ground. Many people immediately made various fearful
predictions on the basis of his horoscope; his father's reply to the
congratulations of family friends was ominous – 'Nothing could
be born from himself and Agrippina that would not be a terrible
disaster for the state.' A clear sign of his future misfortune occurred on the day of purification. The Emperor Caligula, when his
sister asked him to 'give the child whatever name he wished',
looked at his uncle Claudius (who was later to adopt Nero when
he became emperor), and said, 'Give him his name'; this was not
a serious suggestion but a joke to upset Agrippina, since at the
time Claudius was the laughing-stock of the palace.

He lost his father at the age of 3; he was left one-third of his
father's estate, and did not receive even that because Caligula, the
other heir, took over the entire property. Then when his mother
was sent into exile as well, Nero, in great need and almost

penniless, was brought up by his aunt Lepida, under the supervision of two *paedagogi*, a dancer and a hairdresser.

A Roman's interest in his children and grandchildren was partly a conventional wish for heirs; but that did not exclude a close interest in how a toddler actually behaves.

### 129  Fronto, *Letters to his Friends* 1, 12

Fronto sends greetings to his son-in-law Aufidius Victorinus.

If we deserve it, Sir, the gods will show favour to my daughter, your wife; and they will increase our household (*familia*) with children and grandchildren, and will ensure that those who have been and will be born of you will be like you. As far as that little boy who is your Victorinus as well as my Fronto is concerned, not a day goes by without argument and litigation between us. You never ask for a backhander from anyone for a court appearance or speech; but the one word your little Fronto continually and repeatedly gives mouth to is 'Give me!' (*da*). I hand over whatever I can, writing-paper or tablets; these are the things I would like him to make a habit of asking for. He shows some signs of his grandfather's character as well: he is particularly greedy for grapes. That was the first solid food he sucked down, and almost for entire days he kept licking at a grape or kissing it with his lips or biting it with his gums or playing with it. He is also particularly keen on little birds: he loves young chicks, pigeons and sparrows. I have often heard from those who were once my own tutors or teachers that right from my earliest childhood, I too was enthralled by these birds. . . .

### Growing up

While Roman adults were quite capable of describing the actual behaviour of children, some of them also expressed great pleasure at precocious scholarship, as an aid towards recognition as adults (Wiedemann, ACRE, ch. 5). For boys, the putting on of the adult toga, the *toga virilis*, represented the end of childhood, as marriage did for girls. That these rituals marked, in a sense, the assumption of an individual identity is indicated by a quotation preserved by the late republican scholar Varro: 'Scaevola (consul 95 BC) tells us that it used to be the custom for boys not to use their *praenomen* before they put on the adult toga, and for girls not before they were married' (*Auctor de praenominibus*, para. 3.6 = Funaioli, *Grammaticae Romanae Fragmenta* (Leipzig, 1907), 331). Roman law allowed girls to be betrothed 'as soon as they were of an age to understand', though they could not actually marry until they were 12. If a female died before her wedding, her life was thought to be as good as wasted.

### 130  Pliny, *Letters* 5, 16.1–6

It grieves me to write to you with news of the death of our friend Fundanus's younger daughter. I have never seen any girl more playful, more lovable and worthy not just of a longer life, but of immortality. She had not yet completed her fourteenth year,[1] yet she had the prudence of an old lady; the bearing of a matron, yet kept a girl's sweetness and the modesty of an unmarried woman. How she used to hang from her father's neck! How lovingly and modestly she embraced us as her father's friends! How she used to love her nurses, her child-minders and teachers as was appropriate to the status of each of them! With how much effort and intelligence did she use to read! How rarely and with what restraint would she go and play! With how much self-control, patience and constancy did she bear her final illness! She obeyed the physicians, exhorted her sister and her father and kept herself going through the strength of her spirit, even when the power of her body had deserted her. Her courage remained with her to the end, and was broken neither by the length of her illness, nor by fear of death – and consequently she has left us further and greater reasons for missing her and mourning her. What a sad and bitter funeral! The moment when death came was even more shocking than the fact that she died: she was already betrothed to an outstanding young man, the day for the wedding had already been fixed, we had been invited to attend. What joy has been turned to such sorrow!

*Note*

1 All manuscripts of Pliny's *Letters* agree that the girl, Minicia, was in her four-teenth year; Pliny himself must have been wrong about this, since her epitaph gives her exact age (ILS 1030):

To the spirits of the deceased Minicia Marcella,
daughter of Fundanus; she lived for 12 years, 11 months and 7 days.

First marriages, often to much older husbands, were arranged through family friends.

### 131 Pliny, *Letters* 1, 14

Gaius Plinius greets his friend Junius Mauricus.

You have asked me to search for a husband for your brother's daughter. This is a duty which you are right to impose upon me. You know how much I have respected and loved that excellent man, the advice with which he supported me when I was a young man, the praise which he bestowed on me to make me try to be worthy of praise. (2) There is nothing greater or more pleasant that you could order me to do, there is nothing that I could more appropriately accept than to select the young man from whom Arulenus Rusticus's grandsons will be born. (3) Such a man might have had to be searched for for a long time if Minicius Acilianus was not available, as though made for the position. He loves me with the friendship that one young man bestows on another (he is a few years younger than me), and he respects me as though I were an old man. (4) For he wants to be advised and taught by me as I was once by you. His place of origin is Brixia, in that part of our country which still retains and conserves much of its traditional modesty, thrift and rural simplicity. (5) His father is Minicius Macrinus, a leading equestrian who wanted no advancement; for when the Deified Vespasian awarded him praetorian rank, he preferred respectable retirement to public office (or should it be called political ambition?). (6) His maternal aunt is Serrana Procula from the city of Padua. You know what the Paduans are like: but Serrana is an example of rectitude even to them. He also has a paternal uncle, Publius Acilius, outstandingly honest, wise and reliable. There is nothing in his whole family (*domus*) which you would not be equally pleased to find in your own. (7) Acilianus himself is energetic and hard-working, but extremely self-effacing. He has held the offices of quaestor, tribune and praetor most satisfactorily, so there is no need for you to contribute any election expenses. (8) His facial expression is gentlemanly, his complexion very ruddy and his general appearance is nobly handsome, with the distinction of one of senatorial rank. I do not think that these points should be overlooked; for an attractive appearance is something owed, so to speak, in return for a girl's chastity. (9) I don't know whether I should add that his father is extremely wealthy; for when I think of you, for whom we are seeking a son-in-law, then I think that I should say nothing about money; but when I consider everyone else's standards, not to mention the property-qualifications set by our laws, which consider that a man's census-qualification matters more than anything, then I think that this should not be left unsaid. Certainly anyone thinking of their children and descendants has to assess this too when choosing a husband. (10) Maybe you think that because of my love for him I have gone further than reality permits. But I promise you by my honour that you will find that everything will be even better than I have painted it. I am deeply fond of the young man, as he deserves; but one of the things you must do if you are fond of someone is not to overload him with praise. Keep well.

For males, the ceremonial donning of the white adult toga which accompanied the entry of the boy's name into the register of citizens of fighting age was an important event which marked the attainment of adulthood (cf. ILS 1125 = CIL VI,1504, a commemoration by a slave of his master's donning of the adult toga). But if the new citizen's father was still alive, he continued to be in his *potestas* as far as private affairs were concerned.

### 132   ILS 1083 = CIL X, 7346 (Thermae, Sicily)

To the Patrician Titianus, son of Gaius Maesius Titianus and Fonteia Frontina, both of consular rank; Clodius Rufus, Roman *eques*, [presented this] to his peerless friend, on the occasion of donning the adult toga (*ob honorem togae virilis*).

## School and discipline

That the appropriate way of disciplining children was by beating them was so much taken for granted in Greek and Roman antiquity that 'being beaten' became synonymous with 'going to school'. For further literary examples, see Wiedemann, ACRE, 28ff.

### 133 Martial, *Epigrams* 9, 68

What's your quarrel with me, horrible schoolteacher, hateful to boys and unmarried girls? The cocks with their combs have not yet broken the silence, and already your threatening grumbles and beatings thunder. The noise is as loud as that of bronze being beaten on an anvil when a smith makes an equestrian statue for some orator; the applause in the amphitheatre is more restrained when the supporters cheer a victorious gladiator. We neighbours do not ask to be allowed to sleep all night long; to be woken up may not matter, but to be kept awake is terrible. Let your pupils go. Will you accept as much money to keep quiet as you take to scream and chatter?

### 134 Seneca, *On Anger* 2, 21.1–6

It is extremely important that children should be brought up properly from the start, although training them is no easy matter. Although we should not restrict the development of their personality, they must not be allowed to have tantrums. . . . Freedom that is unrestricted results in a character that is unbearable; total restriction leads to a servile character. A child will be encouraged to gain self-confidence by being praised; on the other hand too much praise makes him over-confident and irascible. We should follow the mean in bringing up children: sometimes the child must be held back, sometimes encouraged. He should not be humiliated or subjected to servile treatment. He must not be allowed to cry and ask for rewards, nor should such behaviour gain him anything; rewards should be given only if he has been good, or promises to be good. When he is competing with others of the same age, he should neither be allowed to give up, nor to lose his temper. . . . If he wins a game or does something remarkable, he should be praised, but not to excess: for excessive pleasure leads to over-confidence, and over-confidence to pride. Children should be left some free time, but that should not be allowed to turn into idleness; a child must not be allowed to get used to living an inactive and easy life. . . . If a child has always been given everything he asked for, if his anxious mother always comforted him when he cried, if his child-minder always let him do what he wanted, then he will never be able to cope with anything unpleasant in life.

This stern attitude towards the treatment of children cannot be explained simply as the result of insufficient affection on the part of adults, or of the comparatively high levels of violence tolerated by a culture which engaged in warfare abroad, and watched gladiatorial games as a pastime. Rather, it has to be seen as a consequence of the emphasis on the authority of the *paterfamilias* as the man who, until his death, was responsible for the efficient functioning of the household as the basic unit of economic production. Philosophers legitimate that attitude by arguing that violence was in fact the appropriate way in which rational human beings could control the impulses of those who were only partially rational: barbarians, slaves, children and animals. Seneca argues that the 'wise man', the Stoic sage, cannot really be hurt by the misbehaviour of those who are less rational than himself – but that will not stop him from trying to control such people, if necessary by applying force, as against animals.

## 135  Seneca, *The Constancy of the Wise Man* 11.2, 12

(11.2)  The Latin word for insolence (*contumelia*) is derived from that for contempt (*contemptus*), since you cannot insult someone unless you hold him in contempt; and no one can hold a greater or better man in contempt, even if he behaves in the same way as those who do hold others in contempt. Thus the child will beat his parents about the head and a baby will tear and dishevel its mother's hair and spit at her, or they will show off their private parts to the other people in the household and show no restraint in using obscene words – but we cannot call any of this insolence. Why not? Because those who act in this way are in no position to hold anyone in contempt. . . .

(12)  The attitude we have towards children will be that which

the wise man has towards those who remain childish even when they are past their youth and their hair has turned grey. Have such men improved in any way, if their sins are intellectual and their errors have become greater, who differ from children only as regards the shape and size of their bodies, while they are just as unstable and uncertain, chasing after pleasure without discrimination, fearful and silent not as a result of understanding, but of terror? We will not say that they are any different from children just because children want to collect knucklebones, nuts or small coins, while they prefer silver, gold or power, because children play among themselves at being magistrates, and pretend to have togas and rods of office and law-courts, while these adults play at the same games in all seriousness on the hustings and in the forum and the Senate house; children erect make-believe sand-castles at the sea side, these men as if they were doing something great, spend their time piling up stones and walls and roofs. Instead of a protection for their bodies, they make something that endangers them. These adults are in error just as children are, but their error is different, and greater. The wise man will therefore indulge their insolence, as though they were just having fun, and sometimes he will admonish them with hurt and punishment as though they were children – not because he has been harmed, but because they have done harm, and so that they should cease from doing harm. That is the way in which we tame dumb beasts by beating them, and we are not angry with them when they refuse their riders, but we control them, so that the pain should overcome their rebelliousness. Now you know the answer to the objection made against Stoics, 'why should a wise man punish those who are guilty of injury or insult, when he himself cannot be harmed by them?'. It is not in order to avenge himself, but to improve them.

It would be fallacious to assume that the degree to which the Romans countenanced the beating of their children was characteristic of all ancient, or of all pre-industrial, societies. It must be seen in the context of the peculiar Roman emphasis on the *potestas* of the head of the household. Peoples who did not directly depend on the agricultural productivity of the household did not need to reinforce the authority of the older generation in the same way. When the Germanic Ostrogoths ruled Italy in the early sixth century AD, their warriors strongly resisted an attempt by Queen Amalswintha (the daughter of Theoderic) to impose Roman patterns of authority on their child-king.

## 136  Procopius, *Histories* 5, 2.6–15

Amalswintha wanted to bring her son up in a life-style similar to that of Roman rulers, and had already forced him to go to an alphabet-teacher. She selected three of the oldest Goths whom she knew to be wiser and more civilised than any others, and ordered them to spend their time with Athalaric. This was not at all acceptable to the Goths. Because of their desire to do wrong to their (Roman) subjects, they wanted to be ruled by him in a more non-Roman style. On one occasion his mother beat him when she found him misbehaving in his bedroom. He started howling and went off to the men's part of the palace. The Goths who found him were very angry, and started to circulate rumours to the effect that Amalswintha was trying to get rid of her son as soon as possible so that she could marry someone else and rule both Goths and Italians in association with him. All those Goths who mattered got together, went to Amalswintha and accused her of not having the king educated in a way that was either to their advantage or his own. There was a big distinction between letters and bravery, and what old men taught would generally result in cowardice and weakness. Anyone who was going to be courageous in battle and win great fame had to be protected from the fear inspired by teachers, and undergo weapon-training instead. They said that Theoderic too had never allowed any of the Goths to send their children to school. He had told everyone that a child who had once been overcome by fear of a whipping would never dare to despise the sword or the spear.

There are many references to the misbehaviour of children in classical literature; it was taken to prove that children were characterised by an incomplete rationality, and legitimated the imposition of parental authority. (For some examples, see Horace, *Ars Poetica* 455f.; *Satires* 1, 3, 133ff.; Scholia on Persius, *Satires* 5, 111f.) An inscription found near

Braga (Portugal) confirms that Romans did not trust their children to respect the sacred.

### 137   ILS 4514b = CIL II, 2402 (Caldas de Vizella)

Gaius Pompeius, of the tribe Galeria, son of Caturo . . . to the god Bormanicus, at his own expense, in fulfilment of a vow.

If you care for your honour, if you want your good name to be respected – then teach your son not to shit against this altar.

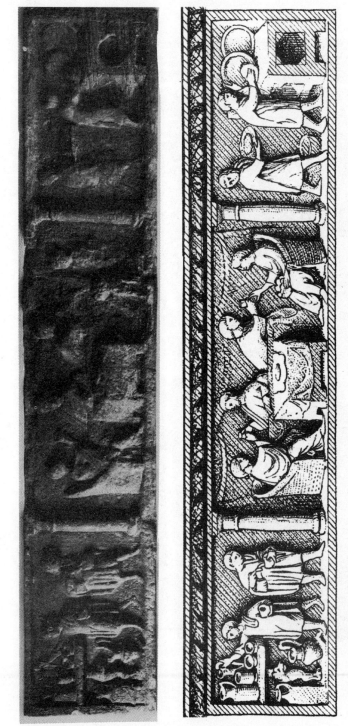

2. Masters and mistresses dine and drink; their slaves serve at table and wash up. Reproduced by kind permission of the Landesmuseum, Trier.

3. A Roman kitchen; slaves at work preparing food. Reproduced by kind permission of the Landesmuseum, Trier.

4. Small bronze vase of a slave holding a lamp, possibly waiting for his master to return home. The frequency of such representations of sleeping slaves may reflect the free population's prejudices against slaves as idle, sleepy and interested only in food and sex. Reproduced by kind permission of the Römisch-Germanisches Zentralmuseum, Mainz.

5. A senatorial woman offers incense at a household altar (for the religious interests of a woman of the same period and rank, see 79). Ivory diptych, probably in honour of the consulship of Quintus Aurelius Symmachus in AD 391. Reproduced by kind permission of the Victoria and Albert Museum, London.

6. Household religion: figure of a *lar* holding a *patera* (sacrificial dish) from a household shrine. Reproduced by kind permission of the Römisch-Germanisches Zentralmuseum, Mainz.

7.   Division of labour: a butcher at work, while his wife writes on tablets, perhaps keeping accounts; Reproduced by kind permission of the Staatliche Kunstsammlungen, Dresden. Herrman-Verzeichnis no. 418.

8.   Tomb of a freedman butcher and his wife from the Esquiline, Rome. The inscription, like the relief, stresses their mutual affection, and tells us that they were once slaves together in the same household. On the left side, the husband proclaims: *Lucius Aurelius Hermia, freedman of Lucius, a butcher from the Viminal Hill. This, my only wife, who predeceased me, chaste in body, who loved me and possessed my loving heart, true to a man who was true to her; we loved each other equally. She never let herself be deflected from her duty as a result of avarice.* On the right side: *Aurelia Philematio, freedwoman of Lucius. While I was alive, I was called Aurelia Philematium. I was chaste, modest, and ignorant of the public. I was true to my husband. My husband was a fellow-freedman. He whom I have lost was much more than a parent to me. When I was seven years old, he took me to his bosom. I came to death at forty. He flourished because I performed my duties well.* Reproduced by courtesy of the Trustees of the British Museum.

9. Dedicatory relief to the north African harvest-god Saturn. Top section: Saturn, seated on a bull, between the Dioscuri on their horses, listens to the prayers of (second section) the donor Publius Novius Cuttinus, with his wife and daughters carrying produce, as he sacrifices a ram and a bull at an altar. Bottom two sections: ploughing, harvesting grain and transporting the harvest. Reproduced by kind permission of the Musée National du Bardo, Tunis. inv. no. 3119.

10. Funerary relief of a Roman legionary, Gaius Aeresius Saenus, and his family, from York. His wife Flavia Augustina is stated to have died aged 39 years, 7 months and 12 days, his son at 1 year and 3 days, and a daughter at 1 year, 9 months and 5 days. Reproduced by kind permission of the Yorkshire Museum, York. RIB 685 = CIL 7, 245.

11. Sarcophagus of a boy called Cornelius Statius, idealising the parents' personal interest in their child: the mother suckles the child herself with the father looking on, and the father holds the child himself. On the right, the boy drives a sheep-drawn play chariot, and recites to his father a poem he has learnt. Musée du Louvre, Paris. Inv. no. MA659. Photograph courtesy of Cliché des Musées Nationaux, Paris.

12.  Two sides of what was probably the funeral stele of a professional child-nurse (an alternative theory is that Anna Severina was a divinity who protected children). Left: suckling; right: putting a swaddled baby in the cradle; Cologne, late 3rd c. AD. Römisch-Germanisches Museum, Cologne. Photographs courtesy of Rheinisches Bildarchiv, Cologne.

13.   A Roman magistrate manumits a slave. Reproduced by kind permission of the Communauté Française de Belgique, Musée Royal de Mariemont, inv. no. B26.

14. Parents and children entertain friends in the dining room. The woman has her arms around one of the two children. The slaves are engaged in activities illustrating their inferior status: on the left, removing the sandal of a guest who has just arrived, and offering him a drink; on the right, giving support to a man who is vomiting. One of a cycle of paintings of banquets from house V.2.4 at Pompeii: now in the Museo Nazionale, Naples. Photograph courtesy of the Ancient Art and Architecture Collection.

# VI

# INHERITANCE

In early times, it had been exceptional for a Roman to make a will, something usually done only in the absence of immediate heirs on intestacy (*sui heredes*). It was expected that the property (primarily the productive land or cattle necessary to ensure physical survival) would pass to the closest relatives. This fundamental principle of many agrarian societies – that land belongs to past and future generations of a family, and not just to those who control it for the present – conflicts with the desire for the freedom to dispose of personal property to whomever the owner chooses. By the classical period, a Roman who had any property to leave usually made a will, in which he nominated an heir or heirs of his or her own choice, and gave specific instructions for the bestowal of the property.[1]

The frequent conflict between a rich man's wishes as expressed in his will, and the social and moral expectation that he would pass his property to his descendants, lies behind many apparent peculiarities of the Roman law of inheritance, as well as behind some of the bitter complaints lodged before the inheritance court (the 'centumviral' court) or, later, the emperor.

*Note*

1 A woman had to have her tutor's consent to make a will; with Augustus's marriage legislation, this became unnecessary for those who had had three children (four for a freedwoman), or had been granted the *ius trium liberorum* ('privilege of three children') by the emperor. Until Hadrian's reign, women also had to go through *coemptio*, a legal procedure to emancipate them from their *familia*, before they were in a position to make a will.

## Inheritance from both parents

All legitimate children, whether from the first or later marriages, were *sui heredes*, with an equal right of intestate inheritance from their *pater*,

117

which, under praetorian rules,[1] took precedence over the claims of other heirs (excepting the patrons of rich freedmen). Children did not inherit from their mothers automatically on intestacy until the passing of the *Senatusconsultum Orphitianum* (AD 178), but it was already common before that for a mother to make bequests to her children. By the time of Severus and Caracalla the child's right to inherit from the mother was accepted, to the extent that even posthumous children not mentioned in a will could bring suit for unduteous will (see **142–9**, pp. 121–5). In the case which follows, Julius Phoebus is careful to specify that his own testamentary requests (*fideicommissa*) are not to be held to apply to property coming from the mother of two of his children. The situation appears to be that she had already died, but any property left by will to her children would, for as long as he was still alive, belong to their *pater*.

*Note*

1 On the Praetorian Edict, see **2**, note 3, p. 5.


**138** *Digest* 36, 1.83 (81) (Paul)

Julius Phoebus made a will and instituted as heirs with equal shares three children, Phoebus and Heraclia (children of the same mother) and Polycrates (who had a different mother). He asked the younger brother Polycrates to surrender his inheritance to the others in exchange for a certain piece of real estate; he also nominated the two born of the same mother as substitute heirs to each other, if either should not take up the inheritance. He prepared a second document relating to Polycrates, with instructions to his mother to open it if he should die before reaching puberty (*substitutio pupillaris*; see below). Then he requested of the older children that if one of them should die childless, he or she should restore his or her share to the survivor or survivors, except for anything received from the mother or grandparents.

Heraclia, the sister, died childless and appointed her brother Phoebus heir. Polycrates had claimed the execution of the testamentary request (*fideicommissum*) in the court of Aurelius Proculus, proconsul of Achaea, and succeeded. On appeal, although Phoebus appeared alone to prosecute the matter, the ruling went against him, since 'survivor or survivors' was held to embrace both brothers. Granted, he (Julius) had substituted only the older two to one another; but this also appeared to be the father's wish, in that he had made an exception of their maternal property, since Polycrates had another mother, who was, indeed, still alive, and who had been charged under a *fideicommissum* to hand on to Polycrates at her death the legacies which Phoebus had given to her in his will.

## Substitutio pupillaris

It was common practice in wills to nominate two or more grades of heirs, as in the so-called will of 'Dasumius' (**158**, p. 134), the lower inheriting if the higher should die before the testator or refuse the inheritance. This was known as 'substitution'. A special form of this was *substitutio pupillaris* (**139**). A child under age (majority being reckoned at puberty or 14 years for boys, and 12 – the minimum legal age for marriage – for girls) could not make a will. Fathers making wills while their children were still under age might provide, by *substitutio pupillaris*, against the eventuality that the child survived and inherited, but then died before reaching an age to make a will himself. This would ensure that the property would not pass by default on the child's death to someone unacceptable to the father (**140**). In effect, therefore, the father was making a will on the child's behalf. It was also common for men to make wills in anticipation of actually having children, and to provide for posthumously-born children in the will. It was usual, though not universal, to nominate the same person in both substitutions. Marcus Aurelius made it a rule that one substitution implied the other in the the absence of any explicit statement to the contrary (*Digest* 28, 6.4.pr.: Modestinus).

## 139   Gaius, *Institutes* 2, 179–81

(179) To our children who are below puberty and in our *potestas* we can not only institute substitute heirs in the way already stated, that is, that if they are not forthcoming as our heirs, someone else is to be heir; but we can go further, and appoint someone to be heir to them, even if they should qualify as our heirs, and should then die while still below puberty. For instance, we can write: 'You my son Titius are to be my heir. If my son shall not be my heir, or shall be my heir and shall die before becoming legally independent, then let Seius be my heir.'

(180) In this case, if indeed the son is not forthcoming as heir, the substitute becomes heir to the father. If however the son does become heir but dies before puberty, the substitute actually becomes heir to the son. So there are in a way two wills, one that

of the father, the other of the son, just as if a son had himself instituted an heir for himself; or at any rate there is one will covering two inheritances.

(181) But, in case there might be some danger of exposing the son to foul play after his father's death, it is common practice to make a substitution of the ordinary sort openly, that is, in the section (of the will) in which the young child is instituted as heir, for the ordinary substitution calls the substitute to the inheritance only if the child does not qualify as heir at all. That happens if he dies while his parent is still alive, in which case we cannot suspect malpractice by the substitute, since as long as the testator is alive the full contents of his will are obviously unknown. But that type of substitution by which we appoint a substitute for the event of the child becoming heir and dying before puberty is written separately on later tablets. These tablets we seal up separately with thread and wax, and in the earlier tablets we make a proviso that the later tablets are on no account to be opened while the son is alive and below puberty. However, by far the safer way is for both kinds of substitution to be sealed up separately on later tablets, since if they are sealed and kept closed up in the way just described, the conclusion could be drawn on the basis of the earlier substitution that the same person is substituted in the later substitution.

## 140   *Digest* 28, 6.2 (Ulpian)

It has become accepted practice that a testator can make a will on behalf of his children who are under age (i.e., up to the age of 14 for males, 12 for females). This applies, however, only if the children are in his *potestas*; we cannot do it for our emancipated children. Clearly we can do it for posthumous children.

A story told by Cicero suggests that the question seems first to have arisen in connection with a will made in the later second century BC in favour of a possible posthumous child. The speaker is Lucius Licinius Crassus (140–91 BC), the most famous orator of the generation before Cicero. Scaevola was not only Crassus's colleague as consul in 95 BC, but also his father-in-law.

## 141 Cicero, *The Orator* 1, 180

Recently the celebrated case between Manius Curius and Marcus
Coponius was held in the centumviral court, before a great crowd
and amid keen anticipation. My contemporary and colleague
Quintus Scaevola (a man extremely learned in civil law, with a
keen intellect and shrewd judgement, and with a polished and
subtle oratorical style – I like to refer to him as the most polished
of the lawyers and the best lawyer among the orators) – Scaevola
stood by the letter of the will and argued that unless a
posthumous child both had been born and had died before
reaching the age of legal independence, the person could not be
heir who had been nominated as heir in second place to a
posthumous heir both born and then deceased. I, on the other
hand, argued that the intention of the testator at the time had
been that, should he not have an heir who reached the age of
majority, then Manius Curius was to be his heir.

## Unduteous will

A parent was expected to nominate his children as heirs, and a will was
invalid unless they were explicitly disinherited. This applied both to
existing and possible future children of the father; Septimius Severus
extended the principle to apply also to a mother's will (145). Even if they
were explicitly disinherited, the law recognised a moral duty (143) on the
parent to make provision for the children, and it was possible, from
about the middle of the first century BC, for them to bring a 'complaint
of unduteous will' (*querella inofficiosi testamenti*) on the grounds of
unjust exclusion. The burden of proof was on the claimant (142). The
'duty' of a son towards his mother, rhetorical and conventional in Cicero
(147), was by the time of Constantine recognised in legal proceedings
(148). Apart from the parent/child relationship, the concept of
'unduteousness' is confined in classical law to siblings from the same
father, i.e., to the *familia* in the narrow sense (149). There was a feeling
that a parent's remarriage might disadvantage the children of the first
marriage (143, 144). By the third century AD (146), it was accepted that
'duty' was satisfied by leaving children the fourth part required under the
*Lex Falcidia* of 40 BC (see pp. 125f.).

## 142 Code of Justinian 3, 28.28.pr.

The Emperor Constantine to Claudius, governor of Dacia. AD 321.

Children bringing a complaint of unduteousness against the wills of parents ought to provide proof that they themselves constantly rendered to their parents the respectful obedience that was their due, as proper human feelings demanded, unless the designated heirs have preferred to demonstrate that they had behaved with ingratitude towards their parents.

## 143 Digest 5, 2.2–4

(2. Marcian:) The pretext under which an action for undutiful will is brought is that the testators were not of sound mind for the making of a will. And by this is not meant that the testator was really crazy or out of his mind, but that he made a will correctly indeed, but not in a way that paid attention to the claims of natural affection (*pietas*); for if he were really crazy or out of his mind, the will would be void.

(3. Marcellus:) To say that a will is undutiful is to allege that someone ought not to have been disinherited or passed over, which is what generally happens when parents under the influence of some mistaken idea disinherit or pass over their children.

(4. Gaius:) We ought not to give in to the wishes of parents who wrong their children in their wills. This frequently happens when they take a dislike to their own offspring, being led astray by the seductions or pressures exerted by step-mothers.

## 144 Pliny, Letters 6, 33

'Drop everything', he said, 'and put away the work you have begun!'[1] Whether you are writing something or reading, have it removed and take up my speech. Like those weapons,[2] it is divine (I could hardly show more conceit, could I?). To tell the truth, for one of mine, it is very impressive; and I am quite satisfied to compete with myself.

(2) It is one I made on behalf of Attia Viriola, and it is notable for the standing of the person concerned, the unusualness of the case and the size of the court. A woman of noble birth, with a

INHERITANCE

husband of praetorian rank, was disinherited by her octogenarian father just eleven days after he had fallen in love with and brought home a step-mother. She was now claiming her late father's estate in a plenary court. (3) One hundred and eighty jurors were in session (the total of the four panels). There was a host of speakers on both sides and crowded benches of supporters, as well as a ring of onlookers, packed together several rows deep all round the most capacious courtroom. (4) The magistrate's dais was crowded too, and from the upper gallery both men and women were craning over in an effort to hear, which was not easy, and to see, which was. Everyone was agog with anticipation, fathers, daughters, mothers.

(5) The court was split over the verdict. In two panels we won, and in as many we lost. It was really remarkable that in the same case, before the same jury, with the same speakers, on the same occasion, there was such a divergence of view. (6) It came about by chance, though it might not seem like chance, that the step-mother, who was heir to one-sixth (sc. of the estate), lost. So did Suburanus, who, after having been disinherited by his own father, had the singular effrontery to lay claim to someone else's patrimony, when he did not dare to make a claim for his own.

*Notes*

1 A line from Virgil, *Aeneid* 8, 439. Vulcan, the smith-god, is being addressed.
2 Those made by Vulcan for Aeneas.

**145  *Code of Justinian* 3, 28.3**

The Emperors Antoninus (Caracalla) and Severus to Januarius; 24 June, AD 197.

If a mother appointed two sons as heirs and then had a third son after making her will, and could have changed her will, but neglected to do so, then the third son, in as much as he was left out without good reasons, could properly bring a complaint of unduteous will. But since you represent the mother as having died in child-birth, the unfairness of this sudden misfortune must be made good by supposing the existence of maternal affection. Therefore our decision is that your son, against whom no blame can be laid save that of being the cause of his mother's fate, shall be awarded the appropriate portion of the estate, just as if she had instituted all her children heirs. In cases, however, where external heirs had been appointed, there is no bar to bringing a complaint of unduteous will.

### 146 *Code of Justinian* 3, 28.6 and 8.pr.

(6) The Emperor Antoninus (Caracalla) to Ingenuus, 25 June, AD 213.

When the question is asked, whether sons can attack their father's will as unduteous, enquiry should be made whether the testator left them the fourth part of the estate at the time of death.

(8.pr.) Alexander (Severus) to Florentinus, 26 January, AD 223.

The wishes of parents when they make a division of their property between their children are not be set aside, so long as a child who knows that he rendered proper duty to his parent obtains by his father's will that fourth part of the estate to which he would have had an entitlement if his father had died intestate.

### 147 Cicero, *In Defence of Cluentius* 45

Up to the time of the trial, Habitus had never made any will, for he could bring himself neither to bequeath anything to a mother of her sort, nor to make a will leaving out entirely the name of a parent.

### 148 *Code of Justinian* 3, 28.28.1–2

The Emperor Constantine to Claudius, governor of Dacia; AD 321.

(1) If a mother brings an action for unduteousness against the will of her son, we order that a careful enquiry be made as to whether the son, without having had any just cause of offence, had offended against his mother in his last will by not leaving her her share (a sad inheritance, but also her right).

(2) If, however, it happens that the mother had beset her son with dishonourable actions and unbecoming machinations, and had laid traps, openly or in secret, to harm him, or made friends of his enemies and in general conducted herself in such a way as to seem to be his enemy rather than his mother, then if this

should be proved, she should accept her son's wishes, whether she likes it or not.

## 149  *Code of Justinian* 3, 28.21 and 27

(21) Diocletian and Maximian and the Caesars, to Alexander; AD 294.

It is useless for nephews and nieces, or aunts and uncles on the father's or the mother's side, to attack a will as unduteous, since no one related in the collateral line, with the exception of a brother or a sister, is permitted to start proceedings for unduteous will. They are not, of course, barred from initiating criminal proceedings on the plea that the will is forged.

(27) The Emperor Constantine to Verinus; AD 319.

Uterine brothers and sisters are entirely barred from bringing proceedings against the will of a brother or sister as inofficious.

## The *Lex Falcidia* (40 BC)

This was one of a series of laws under the Republic aimed at putting some restraint on the divisive effects on landed estates of the common practice among the wealthy of leaving large proportions of their property to persons not their heirs in the form of legacies. The *Lex Furia* (of unknown date) had tried to limit legacies to 1,000 asses; the *Lex Voconia* (169 BC, but in disuse by the late second century AD – see **151** below) directed that, in wills made by persons of the highest census class, women should not be nominated as heirs, a practice which might have tended to take patrimonial property out of the *familia*. It also directed that legacies should not exceed the amount taken by the heirs – note that Murdia, in **157** below, makes her sons heirs, but leaves her daughters only a legacy. By reserving only one-quarter to the heirs, the *Lex Falcidia* gave further scope to those who wanted their property to go to persons of their own choice, notwithstanding the need to hold landed estates together.

It should also be noted that 'heirs' need not be members of the testator's own family. Under Roman law, an heir was in effect an executor, and responsible for debts on the estate. Indeed, as **151** shows, the same individuals could be both heirs and legatees. This apparently rather abstract example in fact represents a common form of will, in which heirs were appointed to all or parts of the estate, and then charged to convey particular portions of real estate or other property as legacies to other parties – as, for example, in the will of 'Dasumius', pp. 134f.

**150  *Digest* 35, 2.1. pr. (Paul)**

The *Lex Falcidia* was passed. In its first clause it gave free power to bequeath by legacy up to three-quarters, in the following words:

> Any Roman citizen who after the passing of this law wishes to make a will giving and bequeathing his money and property to whomever he chooses, shall have right and power to do so, in so far as shall be permitted under this following law.

The second clause set a limit to legacies, as follows:

> Any Roman citizen who after the passing of this law shall make a will shall have the right and power under the public law to give and bequeath as much money as he wishes to any Roman citizen, so long as the amount bestowed as legacy is such that the heirs take under the will no less than a quarter of the estate; and those to whom anything is so given or bequeathed may lawfully take the money, and the heir charged to give the money shall be obliged to give that sum which he is charged to give.

**151  *Digest* 35, 2.22 (Paul)**

Nesennius Apollinaris to Julius Paulus.

My Lord, something like this actually occurred. Titia instituted her three daughters as heiresses with equal shares and gave legacies from each to the other. From one daughter's share, however, she bequeathed legacies not only to her co-heirs but also to persons outside the family, with the result that the *Lex Falcidia* applied. My question is: can that daughter make use of the *Lex Falcidia* against her co-heiresses, from whom she herself receives legacies, and, if she either cannot do so, or could be countered with a defence of bad faith, how then is the Falcidian calculation to be entered upon against the beneficiaries outside the family?

(Paul's reply is that the heirs, in calculating whether they receive a fourth of the estate, in comparison with the amount left to the external heirs, cannot simply charge against their own portions everything that they have to give co-heirs as legacies, but have also to take into account what they are receiving as legacies.)

## Inheritance in some unhappy families

Sometimes personal feelings might clash with the legal rules. Valerius Maximus (152) stigmatises as 'insane' the will of a mother who discriminated unfairly between her two daughters. Where there was friction between parents or between parents and in-laws, a child (or grandchild) *in potestate* might be made heir, but subject to a 'condition of emancipation': otherwise the *pater* would become the owner of the inheritance (153–5).

'Collation' was required of emancipated children who wished to claim part of the patrimony; that is, they were required to add in their own personal property to estimate the total value of the patrimony before it was divided up (156). The attitude of unemancipated children might depend on whether or not this was likely to be to their advantage.

### 152 Valerius Maximus 7, 8.2

Aebutia, who had been the wife of Lucius Menenius Agrippa, made a will that was absolutely insane. She had two daughters, both equally worthy, Pletonia and Afronia; but, swayed by her own whim rather than influenced by any injuries or services done her by either, she made only Pletonia her heir. Out of her extremely ample estate, she left Afronia's sons a legacy of 20 [thousand] sesterces. However, Afronia refused to go to law with her sister, and preferred to submit to her mother's will and respect it, rather than have it destroyed by legal process. Thus she showed herself the less worthy of the injury done her, the more calmly she endured it.

### 153 Pliny, *Letters* 8, 18[1]

Obviously the common belief, that men's wills are the mirror of their character, is false, since Domitius Tullus has shown himself to be far better in death than in life. (2) Although he had laid himself open to legacy hunters, he left as his heir the daughter (Domitia Lucilla) whom he had in common with his brother, since he had adopted his brother's child. He bestowed on his grandchildren very many extremely gratifying legacies, and likewise on his great-granddaughter too. In short, his whole will is full of proper family feeling and that makes it the more unexpected.

(3) In consequence differing views of the matter are taken all

over Rome. Some call him hypocritical, ungrateful, unmindful, and in attacking him they betray themselves by their disgraceful admissions, since they complain about a father, grandfather, great-grandfather, as if he were childless. Others, on the contrary, praise him for having frustrated the unscrupulous desires of men whom it accords with the spirit of the times to have deceived in this way. They add besides that it was not open to him to make a will of a different kind, for he did not leave his wealth to his daughter, but rather restored to her what he had been enriched by through his daughter. (4) Curtilius Mancius, who detested his son-in-law Lucanus, brother of Tullus, had made the latter's daughter, his granddaughter, heir on condition that she was emancipated by her father. Her father let her go, and her uncle then adopted her. In this way the will was circumvented and one brother, who shared his property jointly with the other, emancipated his daughter but got her back under control, into his brother's power, by the device of adoption, and a very large fortune with her.

(5) In general, it seemed almost to be destined that those two brothers should become rich against the wishes of those by whom they were made so. Indeed even Domitius Afer, who had them take his name, left a will which had been made eighteen years previously and rejected by him afterwards, to the extent that he had had their father's property proscribed. (6) His hostility was remarkable, and so was their good fortune; his hostility, in that he removed from the citizen-roll the man with whom he shared children, their good fortune in finding their father replaced by the man who had removed him. (7) This inheritance from Afer likewise was to be handed on like the rest of the brother's acquisitions to his brother's daughter, for Tullus had been made Lucanus's sole heir in preference to Lucanus's daughter, in order to bring them together.

The will is the more praiseworthy in being composed out of family feeling, loyalty and a sense of shame. In it, moreover, all his relatives are duly rewarded each for their good offices towards him, and so is his wife. (8) She has been left the most charming villas, and a large sum of money. She was an excellent wife and most forbearing, and all the more deserving of good treatment from her husband because of the criticism she received for marrying him. It was not considered seemly that a woman of distinguished family and excellent character, already advanced in years and long widowed, who had previously had children, should enter into marriage with a rich old man so desperately ill that even a wife who had married him when he was young and hale would have found him off-putting. (9) Indeed, all his limbs were distorted and crippled. All he could do with his great wealth was look at it, and he could not even move in bed without assistance. He even – revolting and pitiable as it is to mention – had to have his teeth brushed for him. He was often heard to say, in complaining about the indignities of his physical weakness, that every day he licked his slaves' fingers. (10) All the same, he was alive, and had a will to live. His chief support in this was his wife, whose unstinting care had turned reproach for entering upon the marriage into a cause of praise.

(11) There you have the talk of the town, for the talk is all about Tullus. There is keen anticipation of the sale. He was so rich that he stocked up a large park, on the very day he bought it, with a great many antique statues – he had such a quantity of magnificent works of art lying unheeded in his storeroom.

*Note*

1 For what it has been suggested (R. Syme, 'The *Testamentum Dasumii*. Some Novelties', *Chiron* 15 (1985), 41–63 = *Roman Papers* V (Oxford, 1988), 521–43) may be the actual will of Domitius Tullus, see the so-called will of 'Dasumius' below (**158**). The girl, Domitia Lucilla, became the grandmother of the later Emperor Marcus Aurelius.

One of the effects of the wide testamentary freedom which Roman law gave the rich was an anxiety about 'legacy-hunters': if there was an assumption that those who had cultivated an old man's friendship during his last years would be financially rewarded in his will, then how could he ever be sure that they were genuine friends, rather than merely hoping for a legacy? The relationship between true friendship and legacies left in wills consequently became a rhetorical theme for moralising reflections like the following.

Regulus, a prominent barrister like Pliny, was the latter's *bête noire*. His wife seems to have distrusted him too, since she left her estate to her son on condition that his father emancipated him, so that the boy, and not his *pater*, would legally own it. What Pliny does not mention is that, so long as the boy was under age, Regulus would automatically be his *tutor*, with full responsibility for the administration of the estate. The boy was too young to make a will, and Regulus automatically inherited from him. Being now childless, he at once became popular with legacy-hunters. Regulus's desire for a second marriage was perhaps actuated by the dowry that would accompany it.

### 154   Pliny, *Letters* 4, 2

Regulus has lost his son, the one misfortune he did not deserve. He may not think it a misfortune, though. The boy was intellectually bright, but of uncertain potential. It was possible that he would develop all right, so long as he did not take his father as a model. (2) Regulus emancipated him, so that he could inherit from his mother, and once he had 'sold'[1] him (that was the way people commonly spoke of it, knowing the man's character), he fawned on him and made a show of spoiling him, disgusting behaviour and not at all the customary thing for parents. Unbelievable – but think what Regulus is like!

(3) Now he has lost him, though, he grieves distractedly. The boy had a lot of ponies, both for his carriage and for riding, he had dogs, large and small, he had nightingales, parrots, blackbirds. Regulus butchered the lot around the pyre. (4) This was not grief; it was a parade of grief. It is remarkable how people now flock around him. They all detest and hate him, and they keep seeking his company as if they approved of him and loved him. To say briefly what I mean: to curry favour with Regulus, they follow Regulus's example.

(5) He stays constantly across the Tiber in his gardens, where he has taken up an enormous amount of space with huge colonnades, and filled up the river bank with his statues. He is extravagant, in spite of being miserly, and highly pleased with himself, in spite of his bad reputation. (6) So he pesters the city during the most unhealthy season of the year, and in causing upset thinks there is comfort.

He says he wants to get married. (7) He goes about this, like everything else, perversely. You will soon hear about the nuptials of a man who is in mourning, of an old man. In the former capacity he is premature, in the latter, belated. You ask what grounds I have for making this prophecy. It is not that he himself says so – there is no greater liar – but because it is certain that

# INHERITANCE

Regulus will do whatever ought not to be done.

*Note*

1 There is a pun here on 'emancipate' = release from paternal authority (by a
  process of repeated fictitious sale) and 'mancipate' = sell according to the full
  formality of Roman civil law.

The jurist Ulpian records a case during the reign of the Emperor Marcus
Aurelius involving Tiberius Claudius Brasidas, one of Sparta's two
known Roman senators, his sons Antipater and Pratolaus and their
divorced mother Memmia Ageta. Memmia apparently remained bitter
following the divorce. The age of the sons is not known; if, unlike
Regulus's son, they were legally of age, their father would have no
control over the property.

## 155  *Digest* 36, 1.23(22).pr. (Ulpian)

Scaevola records a judgment of the deified Marcus in court on a
case of this kind. Brasidas, a Spartan of praetorian rank, emancipated his sons. A *fideicommissum* (trust) had been bequeathed
to them by Brasidas's divorced wife, to take effect when they
became legally independent at Brasidas's death, and on being
emancipated they sought payment of the trust. Marcus, having
understood the mother's intention, decreed that payment of the
trust was indeed due. She had deferred payment until their
father's death because she had not believed that he would emancipate them; she would not have deferred it, had she expected that
he would emancipate them.

## 156  *Digest* 37, 7.9 (Tryphoninus)

The question arose: if a daughter who was, along with her two
brothers, heir on intestacy to her father had made no claim to the
estate, being satisfied with her dowry, could she be forced to have
her dowry counted in as part of the estate? The Deified Marcus
said that she could not be compelled to do so, since she was not
making any claim against her father's estate. Therefore, not only
will the sum already given (as dowry) remain with her husband,
but in addition the amounts promised will be exacted from the

131

brothers as a debt on the estate; for she has held aloof from her father's property.

## Some inscriptions concerning wills

This inscription in honour of Murdia on a marble tablet was set up in the first century BC, apparently by a son by her first marriage. The commemorator's father seems to have made provision in his will for his widow, as well as for his son. Murdia now makes her children of both marriages her heirs. She also passes back to her oldest son the property she had received from his other parent, although, apparently, she had received it unconditionally, with no instruction as to how to pass it on at her death.

The text is in CIL VI,10230, ILS 8394 and FIRA III,70. Portions of unknown length are missing at both ends of the inscription (it is unclear what the first paragraph refers to).

### 157   The *Laudatio Murdiae* ('Eulogy of Murdia')

[. . .] of my mother Murdia, daughter of Lucius [. . . .] By their own strength let them make others stronger too, to make them steadier and better.

She made all her sons heirs in equal proportion, and gave her daughter a share as a legacy. Her maternal love was expressed by her concern for her children and the equal shares she gave each of them.

She left a specified sum of money to her husband so that the dowry, to which he was entitled, should be enhanced by her good opinion of him. Recalling the memory of my father (her first husband), and advised by that and by her own sense of what was right, she left me a legacy chargeable on the estate, not to show preference for me and slight my brothers, but because, mindful of my father's generosity, she thought she ought to return to me what she had, by her husband's wishes, received from my patrimony, so that, after preserving it by having it in her *usus* (i.e., usufruct of the income), she might restore it to my ownership.

This behaviour was typical of her. Her parents gave her in marriage to worthy men. Her obedience and honour preserved her marriages; as a wife, she endeared herself by her virtues, was beloved for her loyalty and was left the more honoured for her discretion. Her fellow citizens were unanimous in praising her after her death, since the provisions of her will proved both her gratitude and devotion towards her husbands, her impartiality towards her children and her sincere righteousness.

The praises awarded to all good women are usually simple, and identical; the natural good qualities they have at their command do not require much variety of expression. It is enough that all of them have shown the same behaviour, deserving good repute, and since it would be a toilsome undertaking to seek out new praises for a woman, since the course of her life has less variation, it is unavoidable to use commonplaces, lest any proper precept be omitted, and discredit the rest.

My mother, dear above all else to me, deserved all the greater praise for being the match of all worthy women with respect to her modesty, her uprightness, her chastity, obedience, skill at wool-working, diligence and loyalty (*pietas*); she yielded to none when her virtue, industry and good judgement were put to the test, [showing herself] outstanding or at any rate [second to none. . .].

The following will, made in the summer of AD 108, was recorded on a marble monument set up beside the Appian Way. There are no real grounds for calling the testator 'Dasumius' – the nurse Dasumia may have been someone else's freedwoman (e.g., of Dasumia Polla). He was obviously a very wealthy man. It has been suggested that he was Domitius Tullus (see **153**, n. 1, p. 129). There are problems with this identification; a convincing case for L. Licinius Sura is made out by Professor A. Canto (forthcoming). Many of the points of a typical will are illustrated in this, the longest extant – naming of heirs, substitution, legacies. Several slaves are granted testamentary manumission, and provision is made for the maintenance of certain freedmen and freedwomen. This is done in part by individual allowances, and in part from the proceeds of an estate left jointly to a group of freedmen, and including their late patron's tomb.

The text is CIL VI,10229 and FIRA III, 48, with additional fragments of lines 1–19 in W. Eck, ZPE 30 (1978), 277ff. and E. Champlin, ZPE 62 (1986), 253ff. (restoration of lines 120–4). The text as translated includes some new conjectural restorations of missing portions, made by the editors or privately suggested by Professor Champlin.

### 158 The Will of 'Dasumius'

(i) *Naming of heirs and substitutes.*

[Name] made (this) will. Let the following be [my heirs:
(name), my daughter (?), because she] has shown affection and
(of?) my [. . . to half];[1]
[(name)] most exceptional friend, if within [thirty days(?)] he
[shall promise] that he shall bear my [name] and his descendants
[shall bear it, (heir) to one-third;]
[Domitia,] to one-twelfth [of my] fortune(?);
Dasumia [Polla to one-twelfth];
subject to their accepting the estate within 100 days of being
informed and able to do so. [If they fail to do so, let them be
disinherited.]

In place of my most dutiful [daughter(?), the heirs shall be (the
following)]:
[(name), her son (or daughter), to (proportion); Julia Paulina,]
daughter of Servianus, to one-eighth; D[. . . to (proportion)].
10      In place of [(name),] my friend Ju[. . ., to (proportion), and
(name) to (proportion),] shall be my heirs.
In place of Domitia, [(name)] shall be heir to [one-twelfth].
[In place of] Dasumia Polla, [(name)] shall be [heir to one-
twelfth].
They are to accept the estate within sixty days [of being
informed and able to do so].
[If none of these] accepts the estate, then my slave Syneros [is
to be free and my heir].[2]

(ii) *Legacies and requests.*

[Whoever shall be my heir shall be liable to give to the friends]
listed below that which to each of them by this [will I shall have
ordered to be given and bequeathed].
[To each of the following 5(?)] pounds of gold: Julia Paulina,
[. . .]nus, Volusius Julianus, Fabia Balbin[. . ., . . .] Secundus,
Cornelius Pusio, Atili[. . . A]uspicatus.
To each of the following 2 pounds of gold:[3] Aem[. . .,
Mi]nicius Justus, Fabul[l]a (wife) of Asiaticus, Te[ttien. . .

J]unius Avitus, Pont[i]us Laelianus, [. . . Sem]pronius Cresce[n]s,
20 Januari[us, . . .]us Nepos, Tullius [V]arro, Sat[. . .]nnianus,
Appuleius Nepos, Re[. . .]ustius Acanthus, Fabius Rusticus,
[. . .]cus, the Agrii, Phoebus and Servatus, [. . . Va]lerius
Hermes, Otacilius Or[. . .].

To [. . . (?)Pro]culus the jurisconsult, Ateius M[. . .]nus,
30 Cornelius Senex, the Julii, Threp[tus and . . .]orus my relative,
125,000 denarii [I give and bequeath jointly,] with the request that
he and they consecrate [. . . inscribed with my name]; likewise
that at Corduba they consecrate [. . .] inscribed with my name.
[. . . I wish] that the aforementioned works be carried out at his
[and their discretion . . .] and I request [that they be completed
as written above].

To the nurse Dasumia Syche, [I give and bequeath . . .]
Venugus and Arrus, the fishermen, [. . . also those things which]
she shall choose up to a value(?) in denarii of 100[. . ., also
silverware] for use in eating and drinking, from what I possess,
such as she [chooses . . . also papyrus] or bark accounting-paper
[. . .].
40 [Also I ask that freedom be given to] Sabinus the accountant
and My[. . .] subject to their rendering accounts, along with their
women. Likewise [(name)] the cook and Crammicus [the . . .] and
Diadumenus the accountant, [(name)] the treasurer [subject to his
rendering] accounts, [along with his woman, whom he is to] have
in faithful marriage. I order [. . .] to be stowed in small coffers.
[. . .]

[I give and bequeath the following: to C]olonus the freedman
1,000 denarii; to Dasumia Sy[che the freedwoman . . . denarii,
. . . to (name)] the freedman 1,000 denarii; to Heliopaes the
freedman 1,000 denarii; to Ca[. . . (name/s) . . . freedmen] 1,000
50 denarii each; to Eurotas the freedman [. . .] denarii [. . .].


(iii) *Manumissions.*


[The following are to be free:] Eros, the wardrobe-master, on [due
rendering of account; (name)] the child-minder, on rendering of
account, Pho[ebus]. If in any later writing [I shall have forbidden
that any] of these is to be free, [let him not be free].
[The amount due under public law] in payment of the five per

135

cent tax (on manumissions)[4] [for all of those] whom I ordered to be free, [I wish and] request that [my heirs reimburse to those who shall have paid it].

(iv) *Legacies of maintenance to freedmen.*

Whoever [shall be my heir, let him be liable to give . . . yearly . . . denarii . . . so as to give] bestow and concede, without any [dispute, to each freedman, immediately upon manumission . . . and] in addition 5,000 denarii; and in addition [. . . to . . .] as
60  soon as she is manumitted, [. . .] a small coffer, to Thallus the valet, [the afore]named shall give, bestow and concede [. . . to Thau]mastus and Anatellon the freedmen [yearly as long as each shall live at the beginning of each] year for clothing each [. . . likewise to Te]rpnus, Achilles and Heliopaes the freedmen [at the beginning of each year for clothing to each for] each year as long as each of them [shall live . . . denarii . . . likewise to . . . the freedmen as long as] each of them shall live at the beginning [of each year for clothing . . . denarii . . . and that they give accordingly] or arrange that the gift be made.

(v) *Further legacies.*

[Subject to the conditions] written below [I give and bequeath to (name of beneficiary, probably female)] my largest golden [dish
70  . . .] and Diadumenianus the valet [. . .] Stephanus the depilator, [. . .] and Faustus the shoemaker and [. . . of] female slaves(?) of her choice with [their children(?) . . . I give and bequeath to the same] most [dutiful lady] in addition Epaphro[ditus . . .]tus the doctor, Philocyrium [. . . likewise] all my [statues of gold] and silver and [all my] images [of silver . . . and I ask of your] good faith that you see to the public [setting up of . . . the statues of gods and emperors] which I have anywhere, for the greater [honour of my name. I likewise ask that . . . you set free. . .] the steward [on rendering of] account [and . . .]es and Eutyches the older(?) valet. [In addition I give and bequeath to my] maternal
80  aunt Septuma, wife of Secundinus, [my slaves . . . Menecrates, Paede]ros. [I ask that you do not] manumit Menecrates and Paederos, [but] keep them while they live [in the same employment as I did . . . since] through no fault of mine they have so

gravely [offended . . . by injurious] and unacceptable [behaviour].
To Septuma my maternal aunt [I also give and bequeath . . .] the
runner, Encolpius the manager, [(?and property worth)] 6 million
sesterces, which by the kindness [. . .].

(vi) *Directions for the ownership and maintenance of the tomb
and surrounding land.*

[For the preservation of my memory] within two years of [my
90    death, I] ask [whoever shall be my heir or heirs to give] the plot
of ground in which my [remains] shall be interred, [by those to
whom I entrusted the charge that under the terms of this will they
should] inter my remains, to whomsoever [either before the
making of this will or in this will or subsequently] I have given
[freedom], except Hymnus [who has behaved] very badly [. . .
together with the adjacent] woods, in full legal ownership, [on
condition that it do not pass away from their name . . . and that
they do not sell,] pledge, cede or dispose of it by gift. [The share
of any one of these who dies I wish to accrue to the rest, so long
as] one still lives. [But if all of them] shall have ceased [to live],
then to my freedmen's [freedmen, so long as one of them shall
live, I wish the same] to pertain; and if this last shall have ceased
to live, [. . . Since] however [I have divided the ground] into so
many parts and they all [cannot equally] possess the whole that is
100   left [to them . . . I appoint as curators of the estate A]chilles,
Heliopaes, Cym[. . . and wish that by the votes of all who have
a right in it] a curator be substituted for a curator [who has died,
and that by one of them, whom the curators themselves shall
choose,] all the maintenance allowances are to be calculated [and
the yield distributed. In this way the result can be achieved,] I
believe, that through one person [all] derive benefit from
everything.
I request of [. . .] my heirs, [of you in particular, my dearest
daughter . . . not to] allow anyone after me [to be buried in that
place, except those whom I myself manumitted . . . or those
whom you wish in] future of your own freedmen.[5]
Moreover [I wish my monument to be cared for by certain
freedmen . . . espec]ially Thaumastus and Ana[tellon and the
approach and surrounds . . . I wish to belong to all] whom either
before this will [or in the will or subsequently I have manumitted,

110 except you, Hymnus, who, although] I showed you very many
[. . . you yourself recall what] treatment I had or was apprehensive of having from you.

(vii) *Directions for the funeral.*

[My body I commend to the care of] Ursus Servianus, my lord
and [. . . . The bier] I wish to be carried by my dear Servianus's
[freedmen(?) . . . I wish my monument] to be completed by
[(names of freedmen) within . . . days of my] death, at a [cost of
. . . . An account of the expenditure I wish him] to give to my
dear Servianus. [Likewise I wish him to have a stone carved with
a copy of this will] and placed on the side of the monument.

(viii) *Legal formalities.*

[Whoever shall be my heir or heirs,] of him or them I ask and
request [that whatever] legacies [I have made to anyone in this will
shall be paid] to all [without deduction of] the five per cent
(inheritance) tax,[6] [and that they shall either reimburse whatever
has been paid] on account of [the five per cent tax], or on account
of the five per cent tax [they shall] make an agreement [with the
recipient of the item] or compound the matter or [put it to arbitration.]
120 [Anything I leave in notebooks (*codicilli*)] or in any [other]
form, written and sealed, [I wish to be entirely valid, as if] I had
left [them in my will, written] and sealed.
 Any erasures [or insertions. . . .
 May this will be free from all deceit and fraud. For the purpose]
of testation [(name) bought for 1 sestertius my household and]
cash, [scale-holder being (name) . . . and witness Herme]ntidiu[s
C]ampanus. The will [was made at (place) on (day, month)] in the
consulship of [Ae]lius H[adria]nus and Trebatius Pr[iscus].

(ix) *Codicils.*

[Whoever shall be my heir,] I give and bequeath and enjoin [him
to give . . . to the Emperor Caesar Nerva Traja]n Augustus
Germanic[us Dacicus . . .; and to Sos]ius Senecio each [1 pound
130 of gold . . . and] of silver 5 pounds; to Otacilius Or[. . .] the

doctor 10,000 sesterces. Likewise [. . . (property worth)] 400,000
sesterces, from [the yield(?) of which . . .] the freedman Eurotas
[. . . (*two fragmentary lines*) . . .]

*Notes*

1 This and the other fractions in this section are hypothetical; the surviving text
does not supply details of the division of the estate.
2 A provision of this sort was commonly made in case the testator died insolvent
(when other heirs were likely to refuse the inheritance). The slave, called the
*heres necessarius*, could not refuse (though he was not liable to pay the creditors
out of any property he acquired after his master's death), and the disgrace of
insolvency would then be borne by him, not by his late owner.
3 The will originally contained a long list of beneficiaries. The names translated
are those that appear in the central portion of each line which is all that survives.
Some, such as Minicius Justus, Junius Avitus and the writer Fabius Rusticus,
appear in the correspondence of the younger Pliny. The son of P. Tullius Varro
became, after adoption, L. Dasumius P[ublii] f[ilius] Tullius Tuscus (ILS 1081).
4 This tax, one-twentieth of the value of a freed slave, was instituted in 357 BC.
Whether the tax was paid by the slave or by the master seems to have varied
in individual cases. The evidence for the tax is collected in K.R. Bradley, *Slaves
and Masters in the Roman Empire* (Oxford, 1987), 149–50.
5 The conjectural reading in published texts of this inscription excludes *all* burials
of freedmen, but such a provision is without parallels elsewhere. We conjecture
something like (lines 105–6) [*ne pati*]*aris post me quemquam ill*[*o loco sepeliri
nisi eos quos ipse manumisi . . . vel si quos volueris in post*]*erum libertorum
tuorum*.
6 A 5 per cent tax on inheritances was instituted by Augustus in AD 6, to be paid
into a new military treasury fund.

Many shorter inscriptions publicly commemorate provisions requested by
a testator in his will. Like 'Dasumius', this North African had left a
legacy to pay for a construction of some sort consecrated to his memory.

### 159  ILS 3751 = CIL VIII, 18890 (Thibilis, Numidia)

Dedicated to (the divinity of) Successful Outcome:
In accordance with the will of Quintus Julius Libo of noble
memory, by his heirs Annius Titianus Junior and Annius Felix.
Cost: (?) 15,000 sesterces.

An inscription from Alesia in Gaul (the scene of the last and fiercest resistance to Julius Caesar) commemorates a Celtic tribal chieftain, whose career and testamentary details however recall the behaviour of a Roman gentleman. Both he and his wife have imperial names, indicating that they or their forefathers received Roman citizenship, she from Augustus or Tiberius, he perhaps from Claudius. One daughter has her mother's name, an indication of (formal) illegitimacy: perhaps at her birth her mother had already been a Roman citizen, but not yet her father.

## 160 ILS 4682 = CIL XIII, 2873 (Alesia)

Tiberius Claudius Professus Niger
Who held every magistracy among the Aedui and the Lingones, ordered in his will that this colonnade be built to the god Moritasgus, in his own name and that of his wife Julia Virgulina and of his daughters Claudia Professa and Julia Virgula.
His daughter Julia Virgula set this up.

## Provision for widows

Since, by the later Republic, marriage with *manus* had become rare, and virtually disappeared under the early Empire, widows, unlike children, were no longer *sui heredes* of their husbands; they were in fact in the lowest category of intestate heirs. However, husbands commonly made provision for their wives in their wills, either directly as heirs, or by means of legacies. For example, the heirs might be charged to pay the widow an annual legacy during her lifetime (**161**). Sometimes, specially if the children were young, the mother was left the usufruct of the estate (**162**), so providing for her maintenance; or payments might be made to her by or on behalf of the heir so long as she remained with the children (**163**). There might be a *fideicommissum* to hand over the estate to the child when he or she reached a specified age (**162**). A more intimate glimpse of ancient standards of living is given by the legacies of actual foodstuffs (*penus*) and household goods (*supellex*) discussed by jurists (*Digest* 33, 9 and 10).

## 161 *Digest* 33, 1.5; 33, 10.2

(Modestinus:) 'From you also, the rest of my heirs. I ask that you provide to my wife, for so long as she lives, 10 *aurei* a year.' The wife outlived her husband by five years and four months. The question is, whether the legacy falls due to her heirs for the whole of the sixth year. Modestinus's reply was that it is so owed for the whole of the sixth year.

(Papinian:) 'To my wife, besides what she received from me during my lifetime as an annual allowance, I wish there to be given 100 *aurei*.' It would appear that both an annual allowance and a lump sum of 100 *aurei* have been bequeathed.

## 162 *Digest* 33, 1.21.2; 33, 2.22; 33, 2.32.2

(Scaevola:) A man instituted as his heirs his son to three-quarters and his wife to one-quarter, and imposed on his son a *fideicommissum* to hand over his estate to his step-mother. Of her, however, he asked that she should make the youthful weakness of his son her concern and give him an allowance of 10 *aurei* a month until he reached his twenty-fifth year, but that when he had reached that age she should return to him half the inheritance.

(Ulpian:) 'I wish the income from my patrimony every year to be given to my wife.' Aristo replied that this did not pass to the wife's heir, because it was like either a usufruct or a legacy of the form 'due annually'.

(Scaevola:) A man left his wife a legacy of the usufruct of houses and of all their contents, except the silverware, and likewise the usufruct of some farms and salt-pans. The question was, whether the usufruct was due to her of wool of various colours meant for sale, and of some purple, which was in the houses at the time. The reply was that, except for the silverware and the goods intended for sale, the usufruct of everything else belonged to the legatee.

## 163 *Digest* 35, 1.62.2

(Terentius Clemens:) When a man leaves his wife a legacy to be paid annually 'so long as she does not marry away from the children', what is the position under the law (the *Lex Julia et Papia*, which discouraged widowhood)? Julian's reply was that the woman could both marry and take the legacy. But if the wording of the will had been 'so long as she does not marry away from the children before they have reached puberty', the law does not apply, because the condition that is being imposed upon her is rather that of looking after the children, than that of remaining a widow.

## A fictitious will

Writing in the late fourth century, St Jerome mentions a pastiche of a Roman will, a source of much amusement to schoolboys. The text has survived, and may best be found in F. Buecheler's edition of *Petronii Saturae* (Berlin, 1958), 346–7. It shows many parallels with real wills such as that of 'Dasumius' (**158**, pp. 133–9), including instructions for the erection of a tombstone. The will is ascribed to a piglet called Corocotta ('Hyena'), possibly recalling the name of a notorious bandit of the early third century AD. See bibliography, p. 201.

### 164 The *Testamentum Porcelli* ('Piglet's Last Will')

Here begins Piglet's last will.

Marcus Grunter Hyena the piglet made his last will. Since I was not able to write by my own hand, I had it written down to my dictation.

Magirus[1] the cook said, 'Come here, you have overturned the house, you have failed to bury your parents. You runaway pig, I will put an end to your life for you today.'

Hyena the piglet said: 'If I have done anything, if I have done anything wrong, if I have broken any little pot with my feet, I beg you, Lord Cook, I beg you for my life, grant my petition.'

Magirus the cook said: 'Go and bring me a carving-knife from the kitchen, boy, so that I can make this piglet shed his blood.'

Piglet was grasped firmly by the slaves and led off, on the sixteenth day before the Kalends of Lamplighting, when the cabbage-greens are plentiful, in the consulship of Oven and Pepper-sauce. When he saw that he was going to die, he requested an hour's stay of execution, and asked the cook that he be allowed to make his will. He summoned his relations, in order to leave them something from his provisions.

He said: 'To Hoggy Lardy my father I grant and leave to be given 30 *modii* of acorns, and to my mother the breeding-sow Veturia[2] I grant and leave to be given 40 *modii* of Spartan winter wheat; to Quirina[3] my sister, whose wedding I was unable to attend, I grant and leave to be given 30 *modii* of barley. Of my flesh, I will give and grant the bristles to the cobblers, my brains to the quarrelsome, my ears to the deaf, my tongue to the litigious and garrulous, my guts to the sausage-makers, my thighs to the stuffing-makers, my loins to women, my bladder to boys, my tail to girls, my muscles to effeminates, my trotters to postmen and hunters, my claws to bandits. And to the unmentionable cook,[4] I leave the pestle and mortar which I brought with me; he may hang himself by the neck from a rope anywhere between Thebeste and Tergeste.[5] But I want a tombstone to be erected for me inscribed in gold letters: "Marcus Grunter Hyena the piglet lived for 999½ years. Had he lived for another half-year, he would have scored a thousand." You who have loved me best and have been my counsellors in life, I ask you to treat my body with respect, to season it well with the best condiments of nutmeg, pepper and honey, so that my name may be named for all eternity. My Lords and relatives who have been present at the making of my will, order that it be sealed up.'

Bacon-fat signed. Dainty Morsel signed. Cumin-seed signed. Sausage signed. Pork Rind signed. Celsinus[6] signed. Wedding-pig signed.

Here ends the will of Piglet made on the 16th day before the Kalends of Lamplighting in the consulship of Oven and Pepper-sauce.

*Notes*

1 Magirus: the Greek word for a cook.
2 There is perhaps a play here on *vetus* ('ancient'). Veturia is a genuine Roman name (that of the mother of Coriolanus).
3 Perhaps a pun from Quiriniana (a kind of apple) or *quiritatus*, 'squealing'. Quirina was one of the tribes into which the Roman citizen-body was divided.
4 Perhaps a sophisticated legal joke. *Nec nominandus* was a valid way of describing (e.g.) a son one wished to disinherit (*Digest* 28, 2.3.pr.).
5 Thebeste was one of the most distant cities in the south-west of the province of Africa; Tergeste was on the north-eastern border of Italy with Dalmatia.
6 Apicius's cookery book (8, 7.12) has a recipe for *porcellus Celsinianus* – 'piglet Celsinus-style'.

# VII

# MANUMISSION AND FREEDMEN

Although there is evidence that large numbers of slaves were manumitted, this does not necessarily mean that all, or even most, slaves could expect freedom. Slaves in town households (the *familia urbana*) had a considerably better chance than those on rural estates (the *familia rustica*), especially where the latter had little contact with their owners. A number of inscriptions refer to men holding positions of responsibility who were still slaves (cf. ILS 7367 = CIL IX, 3028 = Wiedemann, GARS 152: 'To Hippocrates, manager of Plautus: (dedicated by) the rural slave-family, over whom he ruled with restraint', or ILS 7371 = CIL X, 7041, the tomb of the *vilicus* Gallicanus, who died aged 45, still a slave).

## 165   ILS 3521 = CIL VI, 623 (Rome)

Sacred to Silvanus

Tychicus, slave of our (master) Glabrio, overseer of the gardens, in fulfilment of a vow.

Those with the best chance of manumission were those with specialised skills, who provided their owners with a substitute slave (*vicarius*) to do their work when they got older; and those who were in close personal contact with their masters because of the services they rendered (nurses, child-minders, teachers, doctors, sometimes even hairdressers) or because of personal factors (concubines, natural children by a slave woman, those relatives of freedpersons who were still in slavery).

A peculiarity of the Roman process of formal manumission was that it gave the freed slave not just a legal personality, but Roman citizenship. Ulpian (166), writing in the second century AD, lists for completeness all the types of manumission that had ever been used, although manumission by entry in the census list became obsolete when the holding of censuses fell into disuse in the course of the first century AD.

## Types of manumission

Vindication (*vindicta*) involved a declaration before a magistrate; it was originally modelled on the form of a lawsuit establishing a claim to property, or transferring ownership (Gaius, *Institutes* 2, 24; 4, 16). As **167** and **168** show, this need not take place in a formally constituted court. One party was the slave's owner, the other an *adsertor libertatis* ('advocate of freedom'), i.e. someone (usually a lictor, one of the magistrate's officers) who denied that the master owned the slave and asserted that he was free. The owner would refrain from putting in a counter-claim, and so the magistrate declared that the man was free. The owners must normally be present to make the declaration in person (**170, 171**).

### 166   Ulpian, *Rules* 1, 6–10

(6) Those freedmen are Roman citizens who are manumitted in legal form, i.e., by vindication, by census-entry or by will, and when there is no legal impediment. (7) They are manumitted by vindication before a magistrate of the Roman people, i.e. by a consul or praetor or proconsul. (8) They used to be manumitted by the census when, at the time of the five-yearly review taken at Rome, they entered a census declaration as Roman citizens on the instructions of their masters. (9) A law of the Twelve Tables enacted that those manumitted in a will were free, confirming that grants of freedom are made by will. (10) Those not manumitted in legal form, but given freedom merely by their masters' wish, used to remain in the status of slaves, though the praetor protected their exercise of freedom in practice. Today, however, these people are legally free under the Junian law, which gives Latin status to those manumitted by name in the presence of friends (i.e., a family council).

### 167   *Digest* 40, 2.7–8

(7. Gaius:) It is not at all necessary to manumit at a magistrate's tribunal; so slaves are very often manumitted when a magistrate

is going from one place to another, when a praetor or proconsul or imperial legate has come out to go to the baths or take a drive or watch the games.

(8. Ulpian:) When I was staying at a country house with a praetor, I let manumission before him take place, even though no lictor was present.

## 168  Pliny, *Letters* 7, 16

To Calpurnius Fabatus (his wife's grandfather).

(4) [Calestrius Tiro] is about to set off to the province of Baetica as proconsul, going by way of Ticinum. I hope – or rather, I am confident – that I will easily prevail upon him to make a detour on the way and visit you, if you want to manumit in proper form the slaves you recently manumitted before friends. You need not worry that it will be a nuisance to him; he would not think that a trip around the world would be a long way to go on my behalf.

Under the Republic, an informal declaration made in the presence of a council of family friends (cf. Chapter II, **45**), did not make the freedman a Roman citizen or formally put an end to his status as a slave. In a letter dated November 50 BC, Cicero cancels the manumission of two freedmen, apparently in attendance on his son, who have not behaved satisfactorily. The reference to Drusus (praetor between 120 and 115 BC) is not strictly relevant. We have no evidence about the date of Chrysippus's manumission, and it may not have been carried out at a time when Cicero was a magistrate (e.g., as governor of Cilicia in 51–50 BC). Probably he had merely made an informal declaration before friends, and was now rescinding it. The 'promised oath' in the reference to Drusus may refer to an agreement to provide *operae* (see pp. 152–8).

## 169  Cicero, *Letters to Atticus* 7, 2.8

But that business about Chrysippus (I am less shocked about the other one, a mere labourer – though even he hasn't a match for roguery) – but that Chrysippus should desert the boy without my knowledge! Because he had some little education, I liked his company, I promoted him. I pass over his other misdeeds (and I am hearing about a lot), and his thieving, but I cannot put up with his running away. I have never known anything more wicked. So I have followed the example set long ago, they say, by Drusus as praetor against someone who would not take the promised oath after manumission, and I have denied that I have declared him free – especially as there was no one present who could act in proper form to 'vindicate'.

The contradiction between the following two passages is probably only an apparent one, since the second occurs in a chapter of the *Digest* referring to masters under the age of 20, who, even if not minors, might have a *curator* to act on their behalf.

**170    *Code of Justinian* 7, 1.3**

The Emperors Diocletian and Maximian, to Attia.
    The law is unambiguous: a woman cannot manumit by vindication by proxy through her husband, nor can anyone else through an agent.

**171    *Digest* 40, 2.15.3 (Paul)**

(From *On the* Lex Aelia Sentia:) A master may also in his absence make a case for manumission through an agent (*per procuratorem*).

Manumission by will was probably the commonest form of manumission, since it cost the owner nothing. A condition might be required of the slave, usually in the form of giving service or payment of money to a third party, or (in the case of a female slave) producing slave children (**173**), or, as in the will of 'Dasumius' (**158**), rendering accounts. The will or a codicil might contain a direction (*fideicommissum*) to someone to manumit one of the testator's own slaves; this could make the beneficiary the present of a freedman, without having had the costs of maintaining a slave. Alternatively, the beneficiary might be required (e.g., as a condition of a legacy) to manumit a specified slave of his or her own, or to buy someone else's for that purpose (**176**). In the early principate, testamentary instructions became actionable; legal texts give the impression that it was not uncommon for beneficiaries to try to evade fulfilling the testator's wishes (173–5), but the law favoured freedom. Delays or non-performance could have serious consequences for slave families (177).

## 172  Ulpian, *Rules* 2, 1–2; 5; 7–8

(1) Someone ordered in a will to be free subject to a condition is called *statuliber* (provisionally free). (2) Pending fulfilment of the conditions, the *statuliber* is the slave of the heir. . . . (5) If the heir has made it impossible for the *statuliber* to fulfil the condition, the latter becomes free, just as if it had been fulfilled. . . . (7) Freedom can be bestowed both directly, in these words: 'Let him be free; may he be free; I order him to be free', or by a testamentary request (*fideicommissum*), for example: 'I ask, I entrust to the good faith (*fidei committo*) of my heir that he manumit the slave Stichus.' (8) Someone directly ordered to be free becomes a 'dead man's freedman' (*orcinus*); the one given freedom by *fideicommissum* becomes the freedman, not of the maker of the will, but of the manumitter.

## 173  *Digest* 40, 7.3 (Ulpian)

(15) If a slave is given freedom on condition of serving the heir for five years, and the heir then manumits him (i.e., before the five years have passed), he is at once free, as if the heir had made it impossible for him to serve. If however the heir did not let him serve him, he would not at once attain freedom, but only at the expiry of five years. The rationale is obvious. Once he is manumitted, he can no longer serve; but someone who does not allow a slave to serve him can later change his mind, within the stipulated five years. The slave can of course no longer serve for a full five years; but he can serve for what is left of that period.

(16) Again, Julian in the sixteenth book of his *Digest* has written that 'if freedom is given to Arethusa on condition that she gives birth to three slaves, and the heir brings it about that she does not give birth – e.g. by giving her a drug to prevent conception – then she is to be free at once; for what reason is there for waiting?' The same applies if the heir forced her to have an

abortion, since she might have had triplets.

(17) Again, if a *statuliber* was ordered to serve an heir, and the latter sold and alienated him, it is my opinion that he achieved freedom immediately.

Legislation had to take account of cases where heirs failed to carry out requests to manumit slaves, or tried to impose harsher conditions than those requested by the testator. A series of senatorial resolutions from the time of Trajan onwards denied a defaulting manumitter any rights over the former slave, who became the freedman of his original owner.

### 174  *Digest* 40, 5.26 (Ulpian)

(7) Support was given to grants of freedom by a senatorial resolution (*senatusconsultum*) passed in the time of the Deified Trajan in the consulship of Rubrius Gallus and Caepio Hispo in these words:

> If those by whom freedom is due to be conferred (sc. by *fideicommissum*) refuse to attend when summoned to court by the praetor, and if the praetor on enquiring into the case has pronounced that freedom is due, the status in law (of those freed) is to be the same as if they had been manumitted directly.

The third-century AD jurist Modestinus argued that it was unjust for a slave to be manumitted by a third party who was younger than the person envisaged by the testator; the reasoning is that an older patron would have a shorter life-expectancy, so that (if the patron had no children) the ex-slave would be freed sooner of any services he had promised to perform at manumission.

### 175  *Digest* 40, 5.15 (Modestinus)

The man who is to grant freedom under a *fideicommissum* cannot in any way make the condition of the slave concerned worse. Therefore, he cannot meanwhile sell him to a third party, so that he may be manumitted by the person to whom he was transferred;

and if he has transferred him, he is obliged to buy him back and manumit him – for it is sometimes in the interests of the slave to be manumitted by an old man rather than a young one.

Conflict might arise where the testator required his wife to manumit a slave who constituted part of her dowry; although the dowry legally belonged to the widow, it could be advantageous for her to receive it back by direct payment as a legacy, rather than bring a legal action for its recovery (Gardner, WIRLAS, p.107). Was the widow then bound to carry out the *fideicommissum*?

The mention of a *consilium* indicates either that the wife was under 20 years old, or Aquilinus under 30, so that the manumission came under the terms of the *Lex Aelia Sentia* (see **191**, p. 160). It is assumed that the widow will have her male freedman act for her in legal and business matters.

## 176  *Digest* **40, 5.19 (Scaevola)**

(1) A man left his wife her dowry and much other property besides, with a request that she manumit her own slave Aquilinus before a *consilium*. She denied that she was bound to do this, since the slave was her own property. The question is, whether freedom is due. (Scaevola) replied that if the wife wished to have made over to her in accordance with the will not only her dowry, but also the other legacies, then she must be obliged to manumit Aquilinus on grounds of the *fideicommissum*, and he, once free, would take action to secure her legacies.

## 177  *Digest* **40, 5.26 (Ulpian)**

(1) Thus, support is given to grants of freedom by *fideicommissum*, in that delay in carrying them out is regarded as confined to the fact only. Children born to a slave woman from the day on which freedom could have been applied for, are handed over to her for manumission; those born after freedom has been applied for are born free. Very commonly, applications for fideicommissary freedom are made too late or not at all, because of the inertia or timidity of those to whom it has been left, or their ignorance of the law, or the authority or rank of those by

whom it was left. None of these factors ought to be an obstacle to freedom. The view we uphold, therefore, is that the time limit should be fixed as follows: children are born free from the point at which the delay to freedom (sc. of the mother) occurred, but it ought to be said that offspring are manumitted from the point at which application for freedom could have been made, even though it was not. . . .

(2) A certain Caecilius had assigned a slave-woman as surety for a debt. He wanted her to be manumitted by *fideicommissum* after the debt had been paid; but the heirs did not discharge the debt and the children who had been born to her later were sold by the creditor. Our emperor, in association with his father, issued a rescript: in accordance with decisions of the deified Pius, so that the boys should not be cheated of the free birth which they had been intended to have, the price was to be returned to the buyer, and the boys were to be recognised as free-born just as if their mother had been manumitted at the proper time.

(3) Our emperor, in association with his father, also ruled that if the tablets of a will or the codicils had been opened only five years after the testator's death and a child had been born in the interval, in order that a fortuitous delay should not impose slavery on the child, it should be handed over to its mother to achieve its freedom.

## Manumission and the *peculium*

The *peculium*, the fund which a master allowed a slave to manage as if it were his own, was legally the master's property. However, it was accepted that a slave manumitted in his master's lifetime normally took his *peculium* with him, unless it was expressly reserved. When a master died, unless he made a specific legacy of the *peculium* to the slave, it was absorbed into the estate and the slave lost it.

### 178 *Code of Justinian* 7, 23

The Emperors Diocletian and Maximian to Rufinus, AD 294.

You ought not to have concealed the fact that the situation of those freed in their owners' lifetime is far different from that of those manumitted by will. In the former case, the *peculium* is tacitly granted, unless it is taken away; in the latter, unless it is expressly granted, the legal position is quite clear: it remains in the hands of the inheritor.

Some masters exacted payment of part or all of the *peculium* as the price of freedom. From the time of the Emperors Marcus Aurelius and Verus, the state recognised such an agreement as binding on the master.

### 179 *Digest* 40, 1.5 and 6

(5. Marcianus:) If anyone claims that he has bought his freedom with his own money, then he can lodge an accusation against the owner upon whose good faith he has relied, and complain that he has not been set free by him. At Rome he can do this before the urban prefect, and in the provinces before the governors, in accordance with a sacred constitution of the Deified Brothers, but with the proviso that a slave who brings such an accusation but cannot prove it will be exiled to the mines, unless his master prefers him to be returned to him so that a punishment may be inflicted which must not be any greater. . . .

(6. Alfenus Varus:) A slave had made a bargain to pay money for freedom and had given the money to the master. The master died before he could manumit him, and in his will he had ordered that the man should be free, and had made him a legacy of his *peculium*. (The slave) sought advice as to whether the heirs of his patron were liable or not to repay him the money he had given his master for his freedom. (Alfenus) answered that if the master had entered the money in his accounts as his own after he had received it, it had immediately ceased to belong to the *peculium*; but if he had entered it as money received from the slave, until he should manumit him, then it appeared that it was part of the *peculium* and that the heirs ought to repay the money to the man manumitted.

### *Operae*

An ex-slave was generally expected to show a patron and his family 'obedience' (*obsequium*) and to render help in case of need, e.g., by managing his property when he was incapacitated, or acting as his children's guardian. To compensate his erstwhile owner for freeing him, he was also often required to perform a stated number of days' work (*operae*) for the benefit of the patron. An entire book of the *Digest* (book 38) is concerned with such services. Since a freed slave had the same rights to economic independence as any other Roman citizen, *operae* were legally enforceable only if a specific agreement to that effect had been made as a condition of manumission.

### 180   *Code of Justinian* 6, 3.1

The Emperors Severus and Antoninus, to Romanus. 30 December, AD 204.

If at the time of your manumission, services were required of you, you know that you must render them. However, it is usually agreed between patrons and freedmen that something may be given in lieu of service, although patrons cannot require it to be in the form of a money-payment, unless exceptional necessity may induce a demand for payment to support the patron because of poverty. In that case, even if no services had been required, you would have been compelled to support your patron if his own resources failed him.

### 181   *Digest* 38, 1.1 and 31

(1. Paul:) Services (*operae*) are work performed by the day. (31. Modestinus:) When no services have been imposed, a manumitted slave cannot be obliged to render services which he has not promised, even if he has performed them voluntarily at some time or other.

In the late second century BC, it was found necessary to issue a praetorian edict to regulate attempts by patrons to try to impose excessive demands for such services.

### 182   *Digest* 38, 1.2 and 2.1 (Ulpian)

(1.2) The praetor publishes this edict in order to restrain actions for payments imposed as a condition of freedom; for he observed that the exaction of these payments had gone beyond bounds, so that freedmen were being oppressed and burdened. At the beginning therefore the praetor promises to accept lawsuits on services against freedmen and freedwomen.

(2.1.pr.) This edict has been published by the praetor in order to regulate the respect (*obsequium*) which freedmen have a duty to show their patrons. For, as Servius (Sulpicius, consul 51 BC) writes, previously patrons had been in the habit of making very harsh demands upon their freedmen, that is, as repayment for the enormous benefit that is conferred upon freedmen when they are brought out of slavery into citizenship.

(1) Indeed, Rutilius (Rufus, praetor *c.* 118 BC) was the first to proclaim that he would grant a patron no more than an action for services and partnership, that is, that assuming that this had been pledged, the patron would be admitted to partnership (in the property) of a freedman who did not render due obedience.

Subsequent interpretation of the edict detailed the protection to be afforded to the freedmen. The exaction of services was to be reasonable, and not to interfere with the freedman's earning a living, and the patron was to provide travel expenses and, in case of need, maintenance.

## 183  *Digest* 38, 1.18–21

(18. Paul:) Sabinus in the fifth book on the edict of the urban praetor writes that a freedman should supply his own food and clothing while rendering services; but if he is unable to feed himself, his patron is to supply food.

(19. Gaius:) or certainly the services are to be exacted in such a way that he is allowed enough time for earning a living to enable him to feed himself also on those days on which he is rendering services;

(20. Paul:) and if this does not happen, the praetor himself will deny the patron the right to require services. And that is proper, since each person must carry out what he has promised at his own expense so long as what he owes exists in nature. Proculus says that a freedman is obliged to come from a province to Rome in order to perform services; but the days intervening while he is

travelling to Rome are lost to his patron – that is, so long as the patron behaves like a good man and a careful householder (*vir bonus et diligens paterfamilias*) and stays at Rome or goes to the province; but if he chooses to gad about all over the world, no necessity is to be laid on the freedman to follow him about everywhere.

(21. Javolenus:) Services should be rendered at the place where the patron resides, and naturally the patron is responsible for expenses and transport.

No immoral or dangerous services could be exacted.

**184** *Digest* **38, 1.16 and 38**

(16. Paul:) A freedman shall be obliged to provide services in that trade or skill he learned after manumission, if they are of such a kind that, whenever provided, they are provided honourably and without danger to life. They are not always those which were due at the time of manumission. If someone subsequently begins to engage in disreputable work, he is bound to provide those services only which he offered at the time of manumission. Such services are due to a patron as should be assessed having regard to the age, dignity, health, needs, life-style etc. of both parties.

(38. Callistratus:) Those services (only) are deemed to be exacted which may be provided without immorality or danger to life. If a prostitute is manumitted, she is not liable to provide the same services to her patron, even if she is still making a living by selling her body; nor is a fighter in the arena obliged to provide such services after manumission, since they cannot be provided without danger to life.

The patron could not restrict the freedman's right to exercise his profession.

**185** *Digest* **37, 14.2; 37, 15.11; 38, 1.26**

(37, 14.2. Ulpian:) Freedmen ought not to be prevented by their patrons from engaging in lawful business.

(37, 15.11. Papinian:) A freedwoman is not ungrateful because she practises her trade against the wishes of her patron.

(38, 1.26. pr. Alfenus Varus:) A freedman doctor, thinking that he would have many more patients if his own freedmen did not practise as doctors, demanded that they should attend upon him and not do any work. Was that legal? The answer was yes, so long as the services were not those of slaves, that is, so long as he allowed them to have their siesta at midday and to have regard to their health and their decency.

(1) Likewise, I put the question, 'if these freedmen should refuse to perform these services, how should they be assessed (sc. by a lawcourt) in financial terms?' The answer was that the reckoning should be made in terms of the benefit their services provided, not in terms of the convenience derived by the patron from putting them to inconvenience by preventing them from practising medicine.

Ideally, the patron was expected to make use of the freedman's services himself in person and not sell them to others for profit. Exceptions were made where the patron was not in a position to utilise the services directly.

**186** *Code of Justinian* **6, 3.7**

The Emperor Alexander (Severus) to Minicius. 21 May, AD 224.

(pr.) It is not permitted for patrons to receive payment for the services of their freedmen; but if the agreed services are not performed, an estimation of value may be made in order to exact money in compensation for the failure of respect (*obsequium*).

(1) However, someone who has had two sons *in potestate*, though not necessarily simultaneously, is under the Julian law on marriages exempt from the obligation of service.

**187** *Digest* **38, 1.25 and 27 (Julian)**

(25.pr.) A patron who hires out his freedman's services is not automatically to be regarded as deriving a profit from him; this is to be interpreted with regard to the nature of the services and of the individual patron and freedman.

(1) If, for example, someone has a freedman who is a pantomime or a mime actor, but has himself only modest means, so that he could not make use of the man's services otherwise than by hiring them out, he is to be deemed to be exacting services rather than deriving a profit. (2) Likewise, many doctors have slaves trained in the same skill whom they make freedmen, and they can go on using their services continually only if they hire them out. The same is true of other craftsmen as well.

(3) But someone who can make use of his freedman's services and prefers to get cash for them by hiring him out, that man is to be regarded as deriving a profit from his freedman's services. (4) Sometimes patrons hire out the services at the request of their freedmen; in that case they should be considered to be taking cash in lieu (of the service), rather than a profit. . . .

(27) If a freedman is a professional pantomimist, it is true that he ought to provide his services free, not only to his patron himself but also to the shows put on by his patron's friends, just as a freedman who practises medicine will give free treatment to his patron's friends. For a patron, in order to make use of the services of his own freedmen, is not obliged to be constantly putting on shows, or constantly ill.


Special care was taken not to offend social propriety in requiring services from freedwomen who had attained a high status (e.g., through marriage).


**188** *Digest* **38, 1.34; 35; 46; 48**

(34. Pomponius:) If a freedwoman who has promised services attains such a social position that it is not seemly for her to perform services for her patron, *ipso iure* they are to be cancelled.

(35. Paul, on the *Lex Julia et Papia*:) A freedwoman over the age of 50 is not compelled to provide services for her patron.

157

(46. Valens:) It is agreed that no claim for services should be granted against a freedwoman living as her patron's concubine, just as if she were married to him.

(48. Hermogenianus:) A patron, and likewise the son, grandson and great-grandson of a patron, who has consented to the marriage of his freedwoman loses the right to services; for the woman to whose marriage he consented ought to be looking after her husband alone. . . . But a patroness, and likewise the daughter, granddaughter and great-granddaughter of a patron, is allowed to exact services, since it is not unseemly even for a married freedwoman to render services to them.

## 189   *Code of Justinian* 6, 3.9

The Emperor Alexander (Severus) to Laetorius. 20 February, AD 225.

You have exalted the status of your freedwoman by marrying her, and therefore she ought not to be obliged to render you services, since you can be satisfied with the benefit of the law, for without your consent she cannot lawfully marry anyone else.

Augustan legislation to encourage child-rearing rewarded freedmen with families by cancelling *operae* (see **188** above).

## 190   *Digest* 38, 1.37 (Paul, on the *Lex Julia et Papia*)

(pr.) The freedman who shall have two or more male or female children born to him *in potestate* (except one who has been an actor or hired out his services to fight wild beasts) is not obliged to do, give or perform any work as a gift or service or anything else which he has sworn, promised or bound himself to do for his patron or patroness or their children in return for freedom.

(1) And if he has not two *in potestate* at the same time, but one of 5 years' age, he will be freed from his obligations.

### Augustan legislation on manumission

Slaves formally manumitted became Roman citizens. In the reign of the

Emperor Augustus, legislation was passed to control the quality, and to some extent the quantity, of persons being admitted in this way to the citizen body. The *Lex Fufia Caninia* (2 BC) limited the numbers who could be manumitted by will. This would affect only indirectly the total numbers manumitted; the intention may have been to keep down the proportion of ex-slaves who had no obligations to a living patron. The *Lex Aelia Sentia* (AD 4) applied both to manumission in the owner's lifetime and by will. Criminals were to be excluded entirely from citizenship and banned from the vicinity of Rome. Freedom, but not citizenship, might be accorded to slaves manumitted under the age of 30, or by owners under the age of 20. The lower age limits set for owner and slave were meant to ensure that the slave, on a mature judgement, deserved freedom; exceptions might be made, on submission to a tribunal, for certain cases involving close personal service or actual blood relationship to the owner, or for marriage to a patron. A *Lex Junia* (probably under Tiberius) gave those who did not meet these conditions 'Latin' status and access to citizenship once they had a 1-year-old child, born in a matrimonial relationship (paragraph 29 below, and **196**). Later legislation (paragraphs 32b–4) granted citizenship as a reward for various sorts of public service.

### 191  Gaius, *Institutes* 1, 12–19, 28–30, 36–44

(12) Freedmen belong to one of three status-groups: they are either Roman citizens, or Latins, or subjects (*dediticii*). Let us look at each status-group separately, beginning with subjects.

(13) The *Lex Aelia Sentia* requires that any slaves who have been put in chains as a punishment by their masters or have been branded (or tattooed) or interrogated under torture about some crime of which they were found to be guilty; and any who have been handed over to fight as gladiators or with wild beasts, or have belonged to a troupe of gladiators or been imprisoned; should, if the same owner or any subsequent owner manumits them, become free men of the same status as subject foreigners (*peregrini dediticii*). (14) 'Subject foreigners' is the name given to those who had once fought a regular war against the Roman people, were defeated and gave themselves up. (15) We will never accept that slaves who have suffered a disgrace of this kind can become either Roman citizens or Latins (whatever the procedure of manumission, and whatever their age at the time, even if they were in their masters' full ownership): we consider that they

should have the status of subjects forever.

(16) But if a slave has suffered no such disgrace, he sometimes becomes a Roman citizen when he is manumitted, and sometimes a Latin. (17) A slave becomes a Roman citizen if he fulfils the following three conditions. He must be over 30 years of age; his master must own him by Quiritary right;[1] and he must be set free by a just and legitimate form of manumission, i.e., by the rod (*vindicta*) or by census-entry or by will. If any of these conditions is not met, he will become a Latin.

(18) The condition about the age of the slave first appeared in the *Lex Aelia Sentia*. That law does not permit slaves below 30 to become Roman citizens on manumission unless they have been freed by the rod after a council[2] accepted that there was just reason for the manumission. (19) A just reason for manumission exists when, for example, a man manumits in the presence of a council a natural son, daughter, brother or sister; or a child he has brought up (*alumnus*), or his child-minder (*paedagogus*), or a slave whom he wants to employ as his manager or a slave girl whom he intends to marry. . . .

(28) There are many ways in which (Junian) Latins can become Roman citizens. (29) First of all there are the regulations laid down by the *Lex Aelia Sentia*. Should anyone under 30 who has been manumitted and has become a Latin take a wife who is either a Roman citizen or a woman of the same status as himself (the marriage being witnessed by not less than seven adult Roman citizens) and have a son; then, when that son becomes 1 year old, he has the right under this law to go to the praetor or provincial governor and prove that he has married in accordance with the terms of the *Lex Aelia Sentia*, and has a son. If the magistrate before whom the case is heard finds that the facts are as stated, then both the Latin himself and his wife (if she is of the same status) and son (if he is of the same status too) must be recognised as Roman citizens. (30) I add 'if he is of the same status too' with respect to the son because if the wife of a Latin is a Roman citizen, then her son is born as a Roman citizen, in accordance with a recent *Senatusconsultum* proposed by the Deified Hadrian. . . .

(36) Not everyone who wishes to manumit is legally permitted to do so. (37) A manumission made with a view to defraud creditors or a patron is void; the freeing is forbidden by the *Lex*

*Aelia Sentia.* (38) The same law also prevents an owner under 20 from manumitting, except by the rod and after a council has accepted that there is a just reason. (39) Just reasons for manumission exist where, for instance, someone manumits his father or mother, or his child-minder or foster-brother (*conlactaneus*). But the reasons instanced above for the case of slaves manumitted when still under 30 apply here too; and conversely, those mentioned in the case of an owner under 20 may also apply for a slave under 30.

(40) The effect of this restriction on the freeing of slaves by owners aged under 20 imposed by the *Lex Aelia Sentia* is that, although an owner who has reached the age of 14 can make a will and institute an heir and leave legacies, if he is still under 20 he cannot give a slave his freedom. (41) And even if an owner under 20 wants to make his slave a Latin, he still has to prove before a council that there is a just reason, and only afterwards may he manumit the slave informally in the presence of his friends.

(42) The *Lex Fufia Caninia* (2 BC) set an additional restriction on the manumission of slaves by will. (43) Those who own more than two and not more than ten slaves are allowed to manumit up to half the number; those who own more than ten and not more than thirty are allowed to manumit up to a third; those who own more than thirty and not more than 100 are allowed to manumit up to a quarter; and finally those who own more than 100 and not more than 500 are allowed to manumit not more than a fifth. Those who own more than 500 are not allowed to manumit any more – the law sets a maximum of 100 manumissions. If you only own one or two slaves, the law does not apply, and there are no restrictions on your freedom to manumit. (44) Nor does this law apply to those who free their slaves by some other procedure than by will. Thus a master manumitting by the rod or by census-entry or informally in the presence of his friends may set free his whole household, so long as there is no other impediment to giving them their freedom.

*Notes*

1 Ownership with full legal title, as distinct from *de facto* possession.
2 Not a family council, but an official council. In the city of Rome, it consisted of five Roman senators and five equestrians; in the provinces of twenty local justices (*recuperatores*) who had to be Roman citizens.

A number of inscriptions show the comparative frequency with which a female slave was manumitted in order to become her former owner's legal wife.

## 192   ILS 1519 = CIL VI, 8604 (Rome)

To Titus Flavius Euschemon, freedman of Augustus, who was in charge of his correspondence, and also procurator of the Jewish poll-tax. Flavia Aphrodisia set this up to her patron and husband, who well deserved it.

Liaisons between slaves could not be recognised formally under Roman law as having the force of a 'marriage' (*matrimonium*). But slaves who lived together as man and wife were recognised as *contubernales*. In the following inscription, the term indicates that Claudius and his wife had both been slaves in the same household. Since he is her patron, he may have taken her with him at his manumission as part of his *peculium*, or subsequently bought her from their former owner.

## 193   CIL VI, 15598 (Rome)

To the Shades of Claudia Stepte,
who lived for 72 years. This was set up by Tiberius Claudius Nymphodotus, freedman of Augustus, her patron and *contubernalis*, to his dearest wife, who deserved well of him, with whom he lived for forty-six years. For themselves and their children and their descendants.

Not all such patrons had been fellow-slaves of the woman they manumitted and married: Sarculo was a free-born citizen, and Plutia had been his slave:

## 194   ILS 5010 = CIL VI, 2170 (Rome)

[male portrait]                      [female portrait]
Lucius Antistius Sarculo,             Antistia Plutia
    son of Gnaeus,              freedwoman of Lucius.
of the Horatian tribe,
Salian priest at Albanum,
Master of the Salians.

The freedmen Rufus and Anthus had these portraits set up to their patron and patroness at their own expense because of their merits.

## Proofs of manumission

Formal manumission could be performed in very informal circumstances (see **167**, pp. 145f.), and it is unlikely that magisterial records were kept of what was in form a private legal transaction. For testamentary manumission the will itself could serve as evidence, so long as the document was accessible (see the will of 'Dasumius', **158**, pp. 135f.). Personal witnesses could be called upon. The treasury would no doubt have a record of payment of the manumission tax, although there might be a problem of accessibility and retrieval. In a document from Egypt in the second century AD (FIRA III, no. 6), a freedwoman is recorded as producing in evidence a *tabella* proving her manumission, and there is another Egyptian document (FIRA III, no. 11) recording an informal manumission. This takes the form of a private declaration by the manumitter, with names of witnesses. But the administration of Egypt was unlike that of any Roman province in the strict sense, and no Roman examples of such records have so far been found.

The outcome of the lawsuit in AD 75 to which the following documents from Puteoli refer is unknown. However, the surviving dossier contains no documents certifying either the manumission, formal or informal, of Petronia Justa or that of her mother Vitalis, nor any reference to the existence of such documents.

## 195   Herculaneum Tablets 16, 17, 24

(16) I, Gaius Petronius Telesphorus, have written and have sworn by the Genius of the Emperor (Vespasian) Augustus and of his sons that I know that the girl Justa, who is the object of this suit, was born free, from my fellow-freedwoman Petronia Vitalis, and

that I negotiated with Petronius Stephanus and Calatoria Themis (Stephanus's wife) for them to accept payment for maintenance and restore her daughter to Vitalis. From this I know that the woman Justa, who is the object of this suit, was born free, from Petronia Vitalis; which is the question at issue.

(17) I, Marcus Vinicius Proculus, son of Marcus, have written [and sworn by Jupiter (?) and by the Genius] of the Emperor Vespasian [Caesar Augustus and his sons] that I [frequented the home of] Petro[nius Stephanus, husband of Calat]oria Themis [and patron of Vitalis] at Herculaneum [and that I was present when . . . [(*the next 2 to 3 lines are fragmentary*) . . .] that I heard Petronius Stephanus saying on the 12th/14th day of [(month), about Vitalis (?)], 'The one we intend to manumit, we have [her alone (?)]', and on the Ides afterwards she was manumitted; from which I know that the woman who is the object of this suit was born free, from Petronia Vitalis.

(24) I [(name)] have written at the request of Marcus Calatorius Marullus, in his presence, because he declared himself illiterate, that he has sworn, by the Genius of the Emperor Vespasian Augustus and of his sons, 'That I know that Calatoria Themis manumitted the girl [and] me also, from which I know that the girl is the freedwoman of Calatoria Themis; which is the question at issue.'

In AD 60 and 62, a Junian Latin made a declaration, first of the birth of a child to him and his wife, and later to the child having reached the age of 1 year.

### 196 Herculaneum Tablets 5 and 89

(5) In the consulship of [Gaius Vellei]us Paterculus and of Marcus Manlius Vopiscus, on 24 July, Lucius Venidius Ennychus testified that a child was born to him from Acte his wife.

(89. This text is very fragmentary, but the latter part can confidently be restored to read as follows:) . . . of those from the [number of freedmen who by the *Lex*] *Aelia Sentia* had shown

cause [. . . of Lucius Venidius] Ennychus and Livia [Acte his wife], because [they have] declared that a daughter [born to them] is 1 year old, which is the [point to be established, their case is approved and they are Roman] citizens. The day before the Kalends of [(month)], in the consulship of Publius Marius and of Lucius Asinius Gallus.

# VIII

# BEYOND THE HOUSEHOLD: PATRONAGE AND FRIENDSHIP

As we have seen, Romans were enmeshed in a system of formal obligations to persons on the margins of their *domus*. These naturally included freed slaves (Chapter VII), and close relatives by blood or marriage – though in a society where survival depended on access to productive land, brothers could be rivals for the inheritance of scarce resources, as much as allies against strangers.

But there were other categories of persons towards whom a Roman *paterfamilias* recognised that he had obligations, either inherited or freely entered into by the two parties concerned. These ties could be perceived as being with persons who were formally equals, but who might provide access to goods or services which one of the parties did not in fact possess. Some were quantifiable – a loan, the use of a skilled slave, a dowry for a daughter's wedding. Others were more nebulous: influence in a court of law, support at election-time, appointment to government employment. While Romans were as aware as we are that such relationships were in practice unequal, the fiction that all citizens had the same rights meant that even under the principate, these relationships were described as friendships, *amicitiae*, as if between equals. Where the friendship was between a Roman and a non-citizen, it took the form of *hospitium*, 'guest-friendship'; that formal institution became less relevant as Roman citizen rights were extended first throughout Italy and later the entire Mediterranean. It was only where there were bonds between men or women of different formal status that the term 'patronage' (*patronatus*) was applied: between a freed slave and his former owner, between a Roman and his non-Roman 'client', or between a powerful man and a corporation (*collegium*) or a town or community.

These different obligations might result in conflicts of interest, especially for influential men who would be expected to express their support for one side or another in lawsuits. Roman jurists tried to set up a hierarchy of social obligations.

**197   Aulus Gellius 5, 13**

On categories of obligations, and the order in which they are recognised according to the customs of the Roman people.

I was once present at a debate between men who were old and highly regarded at Rome and outstanding in their learning and knowledge of ancient custom and (legal) science. They were discussing the degrees and order of priority of obligations. There was no consensus on the question of who should have priority and first claim when it was necessary to put one person before another in providing help or being of service. (2) It was of course easily agreed and accepted that, in accordance with the customs of the Roman people, wards who had been entrusted into our guardianship and protection ought to hold the next place after parents; the next place after them was held by clients who had given themselves into our trust and patronage in the same way; then in third place came guest-friends; and after that relations by blood or marriage.

(3) Much evidence in support of these customs and principle is contained in ancient texts. I will just quote the following, dealing with clients and relatives, since I have it to hand. (4) In the speech delivered to the censors, attacking Lentulus, Marcus Cato (the Elder) wrote as follows:

> Our ancestors were not mistaken in considering it more sacred to protect a ward than not to disappoint a client. Evidence may be given against one's blood-relatives on behalf of a client, but no one gives evidence against a client. The foremost obligation is to a father, the next to a patron.

(5) In Book Three of his 'Civil Law', Masurius Sabinus awards the guest-friend prior place before the client. These are the words in the book:

> Our ancestors had the following views about levels of responsibility: first to the ward; then to the guest-friend; then to the client; then to the blood-relative; finally to the relative by marriage. And other things being equal, women are given precedence over men, and the guardianship of children over the guardianship of women (*tutela muliebris*). Even when men have appeared against someone (in court), they have been left as tutors to his sons, and have appeared *for* the ward in the same lawsuit.

167

(6) The words spoken by Gaius Caesar, the High Priest, in the speech which he gave 'On Behalf of the Bithynians' provide firm and clear evidence for these principles. He began as follows:

I am unable to evade this duty, Marcus Juncus, both because of my guest-friendship with King Nicomedes, and because of my relationship [of patronage] with those whose case is being tried. For the memory of a man should not be expunged by death in such a way as to be forgotten by those who were near to him; nor, without incurring extreme disgrace, can we desert our clients, to whom we have undertaken to bring assistance even against our relatives.

Roman 'friendship' was therefore based upon the exchange of very real *beneficia*, goods and services required by the parties involved: 'I give so that you may give', *do ut des*. It was important not enter into such a relationship without being sure that one's partner was a worthy one.

## 198   Seneca, *On Benefits* 2, 18.5

So I must be selective with regard to the man from whom I am to receive a benefit; we must certainly be more careful in our choice of the person to whom we are to owe a benefit than the one to whom we are to owe money. I have to give back to a creditor to whom I owe money what I received from him; when I have given it back, I am released and free from any obligation. But I have to give someone to whom I owe a benefit back even more than I received, and even when I have repaid my gratitude, we still remain bound to one another; for when I have repaid him, I ought to start again from fresh, and the friendship (*amicitia*) remains; and just as I should not receive an unworthy person into my friendship, so I should not receive such a person into the most sacred rights of exchanging benefits, which is the basis of friendship.

Seneca was a moral theorist; but Latin biographies confirm what he says about the obligations and restrictions which *amicitiae* imposed, and the way in which such 'friendship' had to be expressed in the most material terms – promotion to office, and legacies.

## 199  Suetonius, *Augustus* 66

(1) He did not enter lightly into *amicitiae*, and he maintained them most resolutely; not only did he suitably reward a man's virtues and deserts, but he also put up with his vices and misdemeanours, so long as they were not serious. It is not easy to find any whom he turned against out of the entire number of his friends, except for Salvidienus Rufus and Cornelius Gallus, whom he had promoted from the lowest level of society to the ranks of consul and prefect of Egypt respectively. (2) He handed the one over to the Senate to be condemned for treason, and banned the other from entering the emperor's household or his provinces because of his ungrateful and hostile attitude. When Gallus was induced to kill himself as a result of the denunciations of informers and votes in the Senate, Augustus praised the concern (*pietas*) that those who were angry at Gallus had shown on his behalf, but he also wept and bewailed his fortune in that 'he alone was not permitted to be as angry as he wished with his friends'. . . . (4) He himself required corresponding signs of good-will from his friends in return, just as much at their deaths as during their lives. Although he was not particularly keen to receive bequests, to the extent that he never accepted anything under the testament of someone he did not know, nevertheless he was extremely peevish when it came to weighing up the last wills of his friends. He could not hide his disappointment if anyone was stingy in the legacy they left him, or added no words of praise; nor could he mask his joy when anyone treated him as gratitude and proper feeling required (*grate pieque*). It was his custom to return all legacies and portions of an estate left to him by anyone who was a parent, to their children immediately, or else (if they were still minors) to have them returned together with the interest on the day the boy took the adult toga or the girl got married.

A particular benefit would only be given if the giver thought it was in his own advantage; but the institutionalisation of friendship had the effect of obliging the partners to give each other assistance even if the giver would gain no advantage whatsoever from a particular action.

**200 Seneca, *On Benefits* 4, 15.3**

How often have you heard someone say: 'I cannot bear to desert a man whose life I have saved, whom I have rescued from peril. He asks me to speak on his behalf against men of great influence: I have no wish to do so, but what choice do I have? I have already supported him more than once.' Do you not see that this thing has a power of its own, which forces us to perform benefits, first because it is proper, and then because we have already done so?

Such a relationship ideally lasted throughout the partners' lives, and might even be inherited by their children, if it was not formally abrogated. But while Roman friendship was formal, it was not automatic; friends might choose to drift apart, especially if the passage of time made the mutual benefits of their friendship less immediate.

**201 Seneca, *On Benefits* 3, 3.2**

We have considered someone as our friend and looked up to him and admitted that our own good fortune was entirely due to him, so long as the things which we attained [through him] pleased us; then a desire for something different took hold of us, and we turned our attention to that; for it is only human to turn from a desire for great things to a desire for even greater ones. At once we forgot about the things we once used to consider benefits.

The conflict between the theory that all friends, in so far as they were full Roman citizens, were equals, and the reality of different social and economic power, was illustrated by the introduction into Rome of the practice followed by Hellenistic kings, of dividing their counsellors or 'friends' into three categories (cf. Pliny, *Letter* 2, 6). A powerful Roman had so many 'friends' that the pretence that they were his equals could simply not be sustained.

# PATRONAGE AND FRIENDSHIP

## 202 Seneca, *On Benefits* 6, 33–4

(33.4) What – do you think that those lists which your *nomenclator* cannot keep hold of either in his hands or in his memory, that they are lists of 'friends'? Those who come to knock at your door in an immense column every morning are not friends, those who are divided into the first and the second category of admissions. . . . (34.2) It was Gracchus and soon after Livius Drusus who were the first to introduce the custom of dividing their crowd of supporters and receiving some privately as individuals, others in small groups and others all together. So these men had first-class and second-class friends, but never true friends. Can you call a man a 'friend' whose call of respect has to be arranged? Can a man make public his loyalty (*fides*) to you if he slips into rather than enters your house through doors that have hardly been opened to him? How can a man be to any extent free with his advice to you, if he has to take his place in the queue to proffer the indiscriminate and common greeting 'Good day', which even strangers are accorded?

Seneca's series of essays *On Benefits* shows how important the institution of reciprocal granting of goods and services was to the Romans. He lists some of the goods and favours that might be exchanged (see also 4, 15.3).

## 203 Seneca, *On Benefits* 1, 2.4

Help one man with your money, another by standing surety for him, another by applying your influence, another by giving him formal advice, and another with helpful maxims.

The kind of support that a wealthy and politically influential Roman would supply his 'friends' might involve material outlay as well as social support. The veiled warning at the end of Pliny's letter is a reminder that a patron risked damage to his personal standing if recipients of his favour proved unworthy.

**204  Pliny,** *Letters* **1, 19**

Gaius Plinius greets his friend Romatius Firmus.

You are a fellow-townsman of mine, were a fellow-student and have been my companion (*contubernalis*) from the earliest years; your father was a friend (*familiaris*) both of my mother and of my uncle, and (in so far as the difference in our ages allowed it) of myself. These are important and serious reasons why I have an obligation to undertake the promotion of your rank. (2) The fact that you are a town-councillor in Comum is sufficient proof that you have a capital rating (*census*) of 100,000 sesterces. So in order that I may have the satisfaction of your being not just a town-councillor but also a Roman equestrian, I am offering you 300,000 to bring you up to equestrian status. (3) The length of our friendship is a guarantee that you will remember this gift; there is no need even for me to give you the advice which I ought to give you, did I not know that you would do it in any case, namely that you should make use of the status which you have been given by me with all possible restraint, since it was given you by me. (4) High status must be maintained particularly carefully when it has to be respected also as a benefit granted by one's friend. Keep well.

One of the most important functions of a patron was to act as a 'broker', an intermediary between his client and someone else (or the patron of someone else) with whom his client needed to do business. Here Pliny intervenes to help a literary friend, the non-Italian and non-senatorial Suetonius Tranquillus (the author of the biographies of the Caesars, at the very beginning of his career), to buy a farm at a bargain price.

**205  Pliny,** *Letters* **1, 24**

Gaius Plinius greets his friend Baebius Hispanus.

My companion (*contubernalis*) Tranquillus wishes to buy a little farm which a friend of yours is said to have put on the market. (2) I ask you to make sure that he can buy it for a price that is fair, so that he will be pleased to have bought it. For a bad purchase is always regretted, particularly because it seems to be a reproach to the owner's stupidity. (3) In this little farm – if only the price were attractive – there are many features to excite my friend Tranquillus's interest; it is close to Rome, there is easy access to the main road, the house isn't too large, the size of the estate is such as to provide enjoyment rather than take up all one's time. (4) Intellectual landlords such as he need only enough land to be able to rest their head, restore their eyes, walk round the grounds and up and down a single garden path, know every vine and count every tree in the orchard. I am explaining all this to you so that you will be aware how much he will owe me and how much I will owe you, if he will be able to buy this little estate (with all these advantages to commend it) at a healthy price which will not give cause for regret. Keep well.

The patron might try to get a job for his protégé:

## 206  Pliny, *Letters* 2, 13

Gaius Plinius greets his friend Priscus.

You always avidly grasp every occasion of putting me in your debt, and there is no one to whom I am more willingly indebted. (2) Thus there are two reasons for me to decide to approach you rather than anyone else with a request which I particularly wish to be granted. You are in command of a great army, which gives you much scope to confer benefits, as well as considerable time in which you have been able to promote the status of your own friends. Now look to mine; there are not many. (3) No doubt you would want them to be many; but one or two are enough for my sensibilities, and one in particular. (4) This would be Voconius Romanus. His father was a well-known man of equestrian status, his step-father was even better-known; it would be more correct to call him his second father, for he deserved that title by the way he looked after him (*pietate*). His mother comes from one of the first families. He himself recently served as imperial priest of Nearer Spain; you know that that province makes sound and responsible choices.

(5) When we were students together, I loved this man as a close friend. He was my companion (*contubernalis*) both at Rome and in the country; I shared my worries and my pranks with him. No

one could have been more discreet as a friend (*fidelius amico*), more fun as a companion (*sodale iucundius*). (6) There is a striking charm in his conversation, even in his very utterance and expression. (7) In addition he is intellectually gifted, clever, pleasant to listen to, fluent and a brilliant public speaker; the letters that he writes would make you think the Muses themselves spoke Latin. He is greatly loved by me, nor is his love for me inferior. (8) From the time when he and I were both young I have tried my best to do for him whatever our age allowed; just recently I obtained the privileges of a father of three for him from our most excellent emperor[1] – although he makes a habit of granting these privileges sparingly and after careful consideration, he granted me my request as though it was his own choice. (9) There is no better way in which I can protect these benefits of mine than by increasing them, particularly since he himself appreciates them with such gratitude that his acceptance of former benefits makes him deserve additional ones.

(10) Now you know what sort of person he is, what a proven and dear friend to me, I ask you to promote him in accordance with your nature and your means. Above all else, be fond of him; for even if you grant him the most valuable gift that you can, you can grant him nothing more valuable than your friendship. I have summarised his abilities, character and indeed background, in order to let you know that he is worthy to be even one of your most intimate friends. (11) I would provide you with a full-length appeal if you did not dislike long requests, and if my entire letter were not such a request. For the most effective petitioner is one who gives the reasons for his petition. Keep well.

*Note*

1 The privileges of a father of three children were among the incentives introduced by Augustus to encourage large families; they included precedence in office-holding. The emperor was Trajan (97–117), hailed by the Senate as 'best' or 'most excellent emperor' (*optimus princeps*).

Pliny's investment of support in that particular protégé paid off: Trajan accepted Pliny's request that Voconius Romanus be raised to senatorial status.

**207 Pliny, *Letters* 10, 4**

Gaius Plinius, to the Emperor Trajan.

I have the most full experience of your kindness, most excellent emperor, and it encourages me to harness it to the advantage of my friends also. The highest place among them has been won by Voconius Romanus, my fellow-pupil and comrade since our earliest years. (2) For these reasons I petitioned your Deified Father[1] to promote him to senatorial status. But the fulfilment of this wish of mine has had to await your own goodness, since Romanus's mother had not yet formally transferred to him a gift of 400,000 sesterces which she had promised to give her son in a statement presented to your father; on my advice, she has since done this. (3) She has formally sold him certain estates, and fulfilled the other requirements of a formal sale (*emancipatio*). (4) Since everything that had delayed my desire has now been completed, I now recommend Romanus's character to you without any reservation. It is a character adorned by cultivated pursuits and an exceptional sense of filial feeling (*pietas*), which has earned both his mother's gift to him and his subsequent inheritance from his father and his adoption by his step-father. (5) Further points are the excellence of his background and his father's wealth; and I believe that my own requests will add to the weight of these recommendations for your favour. (6) I ask you therefore, my Lord, to enable me to congratulate Romanus as I so dearly wish, and to grant fulfilment of my desires, worthy as I believe them to be; so that your judgements may be a source of honour to me not just in respect to myself, but indeed in respect to my friend.

*Note*

1 The Emperor Nerva, who had been forced to accept Trajan as his adopted son and successor in AD 97.

As well as asking for specific favours, a patron might ask one of his equals to extend his friendship to one of his protégés in general terms. A typical example of such a letter of commendation is one written by Marcus Cornelius Fronto (rhetoric tutor to the later Emperor Marcus Aurelius), to Lucius Hedius Rufus Lollianus Avitus, proconsul of Africa from 156 to 159, requesting that Licinius Montanus, an African who has to return home on account of illness, should be admitted to Avitus's friendship. (Cf. Apuleius, *Apologia* 94f.)

## 208 Fronto, *Letters to his Friends* 1, 3

Fronto greets Lollianus Avitus.

'As I would embrace you on your return' – that oath hazards both your well-being and mine – I love Montanus Licinius so much that I would not easily prefer anyone of those with whom I share the rights of hospitality (*hospitii iura*) to my dear Montanus. On every occasion when he came to Rome he has been with me (*contubernio*); he made use of my house; we always sat down to eat together; indeed we shared and exchanged virtually all our affairs and plans. I would like you to show him as much honour as you would require to be granted to your own friend, companion and counsellor (*hospiti contubernali consiliari*) by another. My friend Montanus is interested in all aspects of literature and high culture, and his learning and eloquence are refined. I realise that I am prejudiced in favour of my own profession, since he prefers nothing to the pursuit of eloquence. . . .to the most eloquent of all, such is your nobleness. . . .

[A gap in the manuscripts apparently described a nervous breakdown, requiring either Montanus or another friend, Terentius Varus, to return to his home in Africa.] So what he asks for is to be able to recuperate by the seaside, and some other reasonable requests. It is not the sea so much as the sea air that he needs. [. . .] I hear the objection that it was only unwillingly and with great regret that he has left my companionship, because despite (?) the chest-troubles which afflicted him, it seemed seriously possible, given the very healthful climate, that he could return from his home-town of Cirta; let us hope so. Since I love him as I do very few others, ensure that you treat him as one who is dear to me; when he is with you, welcome him and win his thanks by looking after him, and give him all the help and friendly advice you can. I hope that you will often find your guest in good mental and physical health.

A patron's obligation to intervene on behalf of his friend in a lawsuit even went so far as to write to the judge asking him to show favour to the party concerned. Fronto explains this custom in another letter:

**209 Fronto, *Letters to his Friends* 1, 1**

Fronto greets Claudius Severus.

The custom of making commendations is said to have arisen originally from good will; everyone wanted each of his friends to be introduced to and made friends with every other friend. Little by little this custom has advanced to the point where even those who are involved in a public or private dispute (and whose case is not disgraceful) are commended to the judges themselves or to those present as their legal advisers (*qui consilio adessent*) – not, I think, to the extent of undermining the judge's sense of justice or diverting him from giving a proper judgment. Since it is an established element of court procedure that after the case has been put character-witnesses should be called to declare their true opinion of the accused, such letters of commendation seem to perform the same functions as a speech of praise.

The purpose of this lengthy introduction? I do not want you to think that I have little regard for your integrity and authority in commending Sulpicius Cornelianus, a particularly close friend, who is to defend himself before you in a few days' time. As I have said, it is in accordance with ancient custom that I am encouraged to write to you in praise of my friend. He is a hard-working and industrious man, of free and generous character, truly patriotic. He relies on the fact that he has done no harm rather than taking it for granted. He is particularly congenial to me because of his interest in literature and polite studies. [. . .] It was not accidentally or by chance that we became friends, and I must admit that I did not on my part seek out Cornelianus's friendship. I had already heard praises of his character, and I have learnt on further acquaintance and from many proofs that it was a true report that reached my ears. We have lived in the same house, studied together, shared jokes and problems, tested our loyalty and our good counsel; in every respect our friendship has been both enjoyable and useful. Consequently I ask to the full extent of my ability that in the trial you should show favour to a man who is most dear to me [. . . .]

Anxiety for my friend has led me to commend him at length; but a guarantee of our loyalty and love is . . . [and I am confident that (?)] what[ever] I request, my whole speech will seem to be but one word.

While some *amici* were social equals, others were perceived as 'clients' in the sense of inferiors. Pliny mentions a conflict between his obligation to deal with his tenants and to attend an *amicus* on the day he enters upon the consulship (*Letters* 9, 37). Notwithstanding the polite pretence that the affairs of such peasants were below the dignity of the elite (**93**, p. 79), the system of patronage required that the powerful should give them their time, as Pliny's description of his daily routine when staying on a Tuscan estate makes clear (cf. the mosaic (*frontispiece*) representing Julius receiving a *libellus* from a tenant).

## 210 Pliny, *Letters* 9, 36

(5) There are occasional variations to my daily routine. If I have stayed in bed too long in the morning or have gone for a long walk, then I go out on horseback rather than in a carriage after my siesta and afternoon reading, since that is faster and therefore shorter. Friends (*amici*) visit me from nearby towns, and they take up a portion of the day (and sometimes come to my aid when I am tired, an opportune interruption). (6) Sometimes I go hunting, but not without my notebooks, so that even if I catch nothing, I will not go home empty-handed. And the tenants (*coloni*) are given some time, though not as much as they think they deserve. Their rustic complaints increase my appreciation of literature and of our urban pursuits.

Inscriptions rarely refer to relationships of friendship between individual families, although we have seen some that give expression to the bond between freedmen and their patron's family (**41**, **194**). But many inscriptions record the responsibilities of patrons towards communities or guild-fraternities (*collegia*): such *patrocinium*-arrangements were recorded on a tablet, the *tabula patrocinalis*. We may note that such patronage might be exercised by a woman, and not necessarily in favour of the same causes as those favoured by her husband: e.g., Livia patronised Samos, but could not convince Augustus (J. Reynolds, *Aphrodisias and Rome* (London, 1982), document 13).

In January 224 AD, the *quinquennales* (highest officials, who were elected every five years to revise the list of town councillors) of Volsinii proposed to the association of engineers (*fabri*) that a statue should be erected to Ancharia Luperca, wife of the leading centurion Laberius Gallus. The following motion was voted on:

### 211 ILS 7217 = CIL XI, 2702 (Volsinii)

Our Quinquennales have rightly and properly proposed that we should co-opt Ancharia Luperca, a highly respected lady, whose character and education are revered, and a woman initiated into (religious?) ceremonies, as a most worthy patroness; to honour Laberius Gallus her husband, leading centurion and equestrian, patron of our association, and in memory of the late Ancharius Celer, her father; and that we should place a bronze statue of her in the meeting-house of our association next to that of her husband Laberius Gallus, so that both her loyalty towards us and our good will towards her be made manifest by being displayed in public; and that a patronal tablet be nailed up in her house.

An archaic second-century BC inscription records the formal acceptance of a relationship of *patrocinium* between the city of Fundi and the Roman senator Tiberius Claudius:

### 212 ILS 6093 = CIL I, 532 and 611 (Fundi)

With the agreement of Titus Fa[. . .], the senators and entire magistracy of Fundi enter into guest-friendship with Tiberius Claudius. We all give ourselves into his trust and assent and select him as our patron. In the consulship of Marcus Claudius, son of Marcus. . . .[1]

> [consc]riptes co(n)se(nsu) T(iti) Fa[. . .]
> [et p]raifectura tot[a Fundi hospitium]
> [f]ecere quom Ti. C[laudio . . .]
> [i]n eius fidem om[nes nos tradimus et]

179

co(n)venimus co[optamus eum patronum]
M.Claudio M.f. . . .

*Note*

1 The consular date referred to must have been at some time between 222 and 152 BC.

In another inscription from the early second century AD, the city of Ferentinum in southern Etruria similarly honours a senator who had been on the commission administering Trajan's alimentary scheme in the region.

### 213  ILS 6106 = CIL VI, 1492 (Rome)

On 19 October in the consulship of Lucius Arruntius Stella and Lucius Julius Marinus (AD 101):

Manius Acilius Placidus and Lucius Petronius Fronto, members of the Board of Four Justices, summoned the Senate of Ferentinum for consultation in the Temple of Mercury. Present to take the minutes were Quintus Segiarnus Maecianus and Titus Munnius Nomantinus.

Since it was the opinion of all that the senator Titus Pomponius Bassus was performing with the utmost liberality the office assigned by the most gracious Emperor Caesar Nerva Trajan Augustus, Conqueror of the Germans, which aims at the preservation of Italy for all generations to come; in such a way that every age-group ought rightly to give him thanks; and that a man of such excellence would be of help to our city; when the question, What should be done? was put, it was decided that the following should be done:

The Senate decides that members of the order should be sent as ambassadors to the senator Titus Pomponius Bassus, in order to ask him whether he deigned to accept our city into the clientship of his great household, and allow himself to be co-opted as our patron, placing a tablet of guest-friendship in his house inscribed with this decree.

Agreed.

Aulus Caecilius Quirinalis, son of Aulus, and Quirinalis [. . .] undertook the embassy.

Provinces as well as individual cities had their patrons, protecting their interests at Rome. Conflicts between different patrons, such as the war between Pompey and Caesar, laid communities which supported one against another open to the charge of ingratitude. The account of Caesar's war in Spain in 45 BC contains a denunciation he made at Hispalis (Seville) for the province's ingratitude towards him after all he had done for it as its patron.

## 214 *Spanish War* 42

From the beginning of his service as quaestor, he said, that province had been his own special concern above all other provinces, and he had bestowed on them such good offices as were then in his power. When he had held the higher office of praetor, he had asked the Senate to remit the taxes imposed by Metellus, and had freed the province from having to provide that money; as soon as he had undertaken to be the province's patron, he had introduced many delegations to the Senate and he had represented them in many public and private lawsuits at the cost of incurring the enmity of many. Although he was absent from Spain during his consulship, he did whatever he could to benefit the province. Both during this war, and in the past, they had shown themselves to be unmindful of all these benefits and ungrateful both towards himself and towards the Roman people.

Pliny had been chosen as the formal *patronus* of a number of different cities, including Comum, where he financed the construction of a number of public buildings and endowed a school (ILS 2927; *Letters* 4, 13; 1, 8; 7, 18; 10, 8; 9, 39). Pliny tells us that he was elected patron of Tifernum Tiberinum when he was a very young man (*prima aetate*): it is indicative of the extra-constitutional nature of such patronage that by the third century AD, women and children often inherited the role (and its financial obligations).

## 215 Pliny, *Letters* 4, 1

Gaius Plinius greets his grandfather by marriage, Fabatus.

It is your wish to see your granddaughter, and myself, again after such a long time. Your wish gives both of us pleasure, and it is reciprocated. (2) For we both have an almost indescribable desire to see you, which we will not put off any longer. So we are already packing our little bags, to make as much haste as the course of our journey will permit. (3) There will be one slight delay – we shall have to make a detour to Tuscany, not so that we can cast our eyes on our estates and family property (for that can be postponed), but so that I can carry out an unavoidable duty. (4) There is a town near our estates (it is called Tifernum Tiberinum) which, with more enthusiasm than good judgement, elected me as its patron when I was still almost a boy. The town rejoices when I come, mourns when I leave and acclaims my public honours. (5) To return its gratitude (for it is disgraceful to be beaten in such affection: *amore*) I have had a temple built there with my own money; and since it is now complete, it would be contrary to religion to put off its dedication. (6) So we will be there for the day of the dedication, which I have decided to have celebrated with a feast. Perhaps we will stay for the next day as well, but that will make us all the keener to continue our journey. (7) May we find you and your daughter in good health. We will certainly find you happy, if we arrive safely. Keep well.

One of the few occasions where private *amicitiae* (other than the unequal patron/freed slave relationship) are referred to on inscriptions was where a tomb was erected by the deceased's *amicus*. One such tombstone, to a man who was probably suffect consul in 191–2 AD, originally mentioned two friends who had performed this duty; one name was subsequently erased, perhaps for political reasons connected with the civil wars of this period.

### 216  ILS 1110 = CIL VIII, 12442 (Vina, North Africa)

To Gaius Memmius Fidus Julius Albinus, son of Gaius, tribe Quirinia, ex-consul . . . (*there follows a list of his offices and honours*):

Gaius Annius Julius Secundus [*erasure of second name*] set up and gave this tomb out of their own money to their exceptional friend because of the outstanding good-will he had shown them.

Finally, there was *hospitium*, the relationship of guest-friendship between a Roman and a non-Roman family. This was formally recorded through the exchange of *tesserae hospitales*, tablets which were broken in two so that each party would be in possession of one half. Again, surviving inscriptions tend to record such obligations only when one of the parties was a corporation or city. The *Lex Ursonensis* (the text of the constitution of the city of Urso in Spain: CIL I(2),594,301.4) prescribes that 'No guest-friendship or tablets of friendship should be agreed with anyone without the agreement of a majority of town-councillors.' Like other kinds of friendship, hospitality implied the obligation to help your friends unstintingly when they were in need, and these obligations were thought to stand even between persons whose states were at war.

### 217 Livy, 25, 18

(4) Titus Quinctius Crispinus had a Campanian guest-friend with whom he had close ties of *hospitium*. Their association had developed because when Badius was ill at Rome before the Campanians switched sides, he had been looked after in a most friendly way at Crispinus's house, with no costs spared. (5) On this occasion Badius appeared opposite the sentries who were in front of the Roman encampment, and asked for Crispinus to be summoned. When Crispinus was told of this, he thought that he was being invited to a friendly and amicable meeting, and he came forward a bit beyond the others, assuming that even when treaties between states had been broken, private obligations remained intact. (6) When they came within sight of each other, Badius said 'I challenge you to single combat, Crispinus; let us mount our horses and see which of us is the better fighter, with everyone else standing back.' (7) Crispinus replied that neither of them was short of enemies on whom they could demonstrate their fighting skills; but he himself, even if he met Badius in battle, would turn away to avoid polluting his right arm with the death of a guest-friend; and he turned to go. (8) The Campanian started insulting the innocent man even more violently as a weakling and a coward, epithets he deserved himself, calling his guest-friend an enemy who was pretending to spare someone who he knew was a better fighter. (9) If, he said, he thought that private obligations were insufficiently broken when treaties between states were rescinded, then Badius the Campanian publicly renounced his guest-friendship with Titus Quinctius Crispinus the Roman in the hearing of both armies.

# INDEX OF PASSAGES CITED

*Numbers in bold type refer to the numbered sources in the text;
followed by page references.*

**Literary texts**

**Augustine**, St (Aurelius Augustinus), AD 354–430, from
Thagaste in North Africa, a philosopher-rhetor converted in
AD 386 to a neo-Platonic Christianity; later Bishop of Hippo
(Bône). Theological treatises, sermons and letters survive.
*The City of God* (*De Civitate Dei*) 4, 11 **33**, 34

**Benedict**, St, of Nursia, *c.* AD 480–547, father of western
monasticism, wrote his *Rule* for the monastery of
Montecassino, which he founded in 529. The Latin text is in
*Patrologia Latina*, vol. 66, 215ff., and *Corpus Scriptorum
Ecclesiasticorum Latinorum*, vol. 75 (ed. Hanslik, Vienna,
1960).
*Rule*, ch. 2 **8**, 11
*Rule*, ch. 3 **24**, 28
*Rule*, chs 36–7 **101**, 90
*Rule*, chs 39–41 **98**, 84
*Rule*, ch. 66 **87**, 74

Marcus Porcius **Cato**, 234–149 BC, censor in 184 BC; attempted
to preserve social stability by asserting traditional values
against the effects of increasing wealth and of Greek culture,
thus coming to symbolise old-fashioned Italian virtues.
*Agriculture* 138–41 **34**, 35

(*Noctes Atticae*) are a largely unsystematic collection of information about Roman antiquities and the Latin language.
5, 13  **197**, 167
12, 1  **121**, 104

**Juvenal** (Decimus Junius Juvenalis), born AD 67, satirist.
*Satire* 13, 70–2  **111**, 97

**Livy** (Titus Livius), *c.* 59 BC–AD 17, wrote a patriotic history of Rome from its foundation down to 9 BC.
25, 18  **217**, 183

**Martial** (Marcus Valerius Martialis), from Bilbilis in Spain, wrote several books of short poems (epigrams) towards the end of the first century AD.
*Epigrams* 5, 34 and 10, 61  **125**, 106
*Epigrams* 6, 28 and 29  **124**, 105
*Epigrams* 9, 68  **133**, 112
*Epigrams* 10, 92  **36**, 37

Cornelius **Nepos**, first-century BC antiquarian and biographer.
*Atticus* 13  **7**, 10

**Ovid** (Publius Ovidius Naso), 43 BC–AD 18, wrote love poetry, a mythological epic (the *Metamorphoses*), and a description of the Roman festivals in verse (the *Fasti*, 'Calendars'; only the first six books, covering January to June, were completed).
*Fasti* 2, 617–34  **38**, 38
*Fasti* 2, 639–56  **37**, 38
*Fasti* 3, 817–20  **84**, 72
*Metamorphoses* 9, 669–81  **112**, 98

Gaius **Petronius** Arbiter, died AD 66, wrote a Latin romance satirising the Greek genre of the romantic novel. Only sections of the original sixteen books survive; one of the best-known is an account of a dinner given by a wealthy freedman (the *Cena Trimalchionis*).
*Satyricon* 53  **5**, 7
*Satyricon* 60  **26**, 31
*Satyricon* 70  **17**, 20

# INDEX OF PASSAGES CITED

Titus Maccius **Plautus**, *c*. 250–184 BC, writer of comedies.
*Rudens* ('The Rope') 83–8, 96–102  **81**, 70

**Pliny the Elder** (Gaius Plinius Secundus), *c*. AD 23–79, soldier and imperial procurator. Apart from lost historical works, he wrote a natural history in thirty-seven books.
7, 13/57, 59–60  **113**, 98
7, 43/139–40  **50**, 47
7, 48/156–8, 162–4  **99**, 87

**Pliny the Younger** (Gaius Plinius Caecilius Secundus), *c*. AD 61– after 112. Lawyer and administrator; published ten books of letters, the last being a collection of his correspondence with the Emperor Trajan (mainly as governor of Bithynia in AD 110–12).
*Letters* 1, 14  **131**, 110
*Letters* 1, 19  **204**, 172
*Letters* 1, 24  **205**, 172
*Letters* 2, 13  **206**, 173
*Letters* 3, 1  **103**, 91
*Letters* 4, 1  **215**, 181
*Letters* 4, 2  **154**, 130
*Letters* 4, 19.2–4  **70**, 62
*Letters* 5, 16.1–6  **130**, 109
*Letters* 6, 3  **106**, 93
*Letters* 6, 33  **144**, 122
*Letters* 7, 16.4  **168**, 146
*Letters* 8, 10 and 11  **117**, 100
*Letters* 8, 16  **39**, 39
*Letters* 8, 18  **153**, 127
*Letters* 9, 15  **93**, 79
*Letters* 9, 36  **210**, 178
*Letters* 9, 39  **35**, 37
*Letters* 10, 4  **207**, 175

**Plutarch** of Chaeronea (Boeotia), *c*. AD 45–120, Greek writer of popular philosophical essays, including moralising biographies comparing figures from Greek and Roman history.
*Cato the Elder* 20, 4–7  **118**, 102
*Cato the Elder* 21.4  **18**, 20

187

*Cato the Younger*, 24–5  **64**, 58

**Procopius**, sixth-century AD Greek historian of the reign of Justinian.
*Histories* 5, 2.6–15  **136**, 115

**Publilius Syrus**, mid-first-century BC writer of mimes for performance at Rome; a collection of moral apophthegms (*Sententiae*) occurring in his mimes was made after his death.
*Maxims*  **49**, 46

Lucius Annaeus **Seneca**, *c.* 4 BC–AD 65, Stoic philosopher and adviser to the emperor Nero, to whom he addressed an essay on clemency (*De Clementia*). He wrote other essays and letters, mainly on moral issues.
*Letters* 12  **109**, 95
*On Anger* 2, 21.1–6  **134**, 112
*On Benefits* 1, 2.4  **203**, 171
*On Benefits* 2, 18.5  **198**, 168
*On Benefits* 3, 3.2  **201**, 170
*On Benefits* 4, 15.3  **200**, 170
*On Benefits* 4, 27.5  **71**, 62
*On Benefits* 6, 33.4–34.2  **202**, 171
*On Benefits* 7, 5.2  **82**, 71
*On Clemency* 1, 15  **12**, 15
*The Constancy of the Wise Man* 11.2, 12  **135**, 113

**Spanish War** (*Bellum Hispaniense* in the Caesarian Corpus), an account by one of Julius Caesar's officers of his campaign against Pompey's son Sextus Pompeius in Spain in 45 BC.
42  **214**, 181

Gaius **Suetonius** Tranquillus, *c.* 70 to after AD 121, scholar and secretary to the Emperor Hadrian; wrote biographies of the emperors from Julius Caesar to Domitian.
*Augustus* 62  **63**, 57
*Augustus* 64  **119**, 102
*Augustus* 66  **199**, 169
*Augustus* 67  **16**, 19
*Caesar* 47–8  **15**, 19

*Nero* 6  **128**, 107

Quintus Aurelius **Symmachus**, *c.* AD 345–402, leading representative of late Roman (pagan) classical culture in the Senate.
*Letters* 3, 20  **120**, 103

***Testamentum Porcelli*** ('Piglet's Last Will'), third- or fourth-century AD school text, widely known in late antiquity.  **164**, 142

Albius **Tibullus**, *c.* 50–19 BC, elegiac poet.
1, 5.19–35  **25**, 30

Marcus Terentius **Varro**, 116–27 BC, soldier, politician and polymath; of his voluminous writings, only three books on agriculture (*Rerum Rusticarum*) and six on Latin philology survive.
*Agriculture* 1, 16.2–6  **80**, 68
*Agriculture* 1, 17  **83**, 71

**Valerius Maximus** produced *Factorum ac Dictorum Memorabilium libri ix*, a collection of historical *exempla* for rhetorical use, dedicated to the Emperor Tiberius between 31 and 37 AD.
1, 7.4  **21**, 23
2, 1.6  **61**, 56
2, 1.9  **102**, 90
5, 8  **11**, 13
6, 3.9  **62**, 57
7, 8.2  **152**, 127

**Vitruvius** served as military architect under Julius Caesar and Octavian; wrote a systematic treatise *De Architectura* in ten books.
*On Architecture* 6, 5.1–2  **6**, 9

### Legal sources

**Digest**, collection of authoritative statements on Roman law by earlier jurists, edited at the instigation of the Emperor Justinian and promulgated in AD 533. Among the jurists cited are:

P. Juventius Celsus (consul for the second time in AD 129), a member of Hadrian's council; Aemilius Macer (early third century AD); Ulpius Marcellus (second century AD); Aelius Marcianus (third century AD); Herennius Modestinus (police chief between AD 224 and 244); Julius Paulus (Paul; early third century AD); Pomponius (mid-second century AD); Domitius Ulpianus (Ulpian, praetorian prefect 222–3 AD); Quintus Cervidius Scaevola (adviser to Marcus Aurelius); and Tryphoninus (*c.* AD 200).

5, 2.2–4 **143**, 122
7, 7.6 **89**, 76
17, 1.26.8 **91**, 77
18, 1.42 **19**, 21
23, 2.1–6; 8–9; 21–4 **14**, 17
25, 3.1 **65**, 60
28, 6.2 **140**, 120
29, 5 **23**, 27
32, 79.1 **104**, 92
32, 99 **86**, 73
33, 1.5; 10.2 **161**, 140
33, 1.21.2; 2.22; 2.32.2 **162**, 141
33, 2.33 **105**, 93
35, 1.62.2 **163**, 141
35, 2.1.pr. **150**, 126
35, 2.22 **151**, 126
35, 2.68.pr. **100**, 88
36, 1.23(22).pr. **155**, 131
36, 1.83 (81) **138**, 118
37, 7.9 **156**, 131
37, 14.2; 37, 15.11; **185**, 156
38, 1.1 and 31 **181**, 153
38, 1.2 and 2.1.pr.-1 **182**, 153
38, 1.16 and 38 **184**, 155
38, 1.18–21 **183**, 154
38, 1.25 and 27 **187**, 157
38, 1.26 **185**, 156
38, 1.34; 35; 46; 48 **188**, 157
38, 1.37 **190**, 158
40, 1.5 and 6 **179**, 152
40, 2.7–8 **167**, 145

**Gaius**, possibly late second century AD; wrote an influential introductory handbook for law students.

**Justinian**, Roman (Byzantine) emperor AD 527–65; responsible for the definitive codification of Roman law called the *Corpus Juris Civilis*, which included the *Digest* and the *Institutes* (a handbook for law schools) as well as the *Codex Justinianus*, containing imperial legislation.

**Theodosian Code**, the first systematic compilation of imperial legislation, compiled in AD 438 at the instigation of the Emperor Theodosius II (reigned 408–50).

**Ulpian** (Domitius Ulpianus), from Tyre in Phoenicia; praetorian prefect 222–3 AD; also the most frequently cited jurist in the *Digest*.

> *Rules* 1, 6–10 **166**, 145
> *Rules* 2, 1–2; 5; 7–8 **173**, 148
> *Rules* 11, 1 and 27 **13**, 16

## Inscriptions

*Année Epigraphique*
> 1971, no. 88 (Puteoli) **22**, 24
> 1973, no.139 (Murecine, near Pompeii) **47**, 44
> 1973, no.143 (Murecine, near Pompeii) **88**, 75

*Corpus Inscriptionum Latinarum*
> CIL I,532 (Fundi) **212**, 179
> CIL I,1007 (Rome) **54**, 52
> CIL I,1479 (Cartagena, Spain) **76**, 65
> CIL I(2), p. 729 (Rome) **68**, 61
> CIL II,1980 (Adra, Spain) **31**, 33
> CIL II,2403 (Caldas de Vizella, Portugal) **137**, 116
> CIL III,3572 (Aquincum/Budapest) **114**, 99
> CIL III,6456 (Aquincum/Budapest) **27**, 32
> CIL III,6759 (Ankara) **116**, 100
> CIL V,4241 (Concesi, Italy) **40**, 40
> CIL V,6896 (Villeneuve, Aosta) **72**, 63
> CIL VI,259 (Rome) **30**, 33
> CIL VI,623 (Rome) **165**, 144
> CIL VI,1492 (Rome) **213**, 180
> CIL VI,1527 (Rome) **52**, 49
> CIL VI,1779 (Rome) **79**, 66
> CIL VI,2170 (Rome) **194**, 163
> CIL VI,2210 (Rome) **107**, 94
> CIL VI,5163 (Rome) **127**, 107
> CIL VI,7595 (Rome) **77**, 65
> CIL VI,8012 (Rome) **73**, 64
> CIL VI,8514 (Rome) **126**, 106
> CIL VI,8517 (Rome) **115**, 99
> CIL VI,8604 (Rome) **192**, 162
> CIL VI,8972 (Rome) **69**, 62

# INDEX OF PASSAGES CITED

ILS 1218 = CIL XI,831 (Modena) **59**, 55
ILS 1259 = CIL VI,1779 (Rome) **79**, 66
ILS 1519 = CIL VI,8604 (Rome) **192**, 162
ILS 1570 = CIL VI,8514 (Rome) **126**, 106
ILS 1583 = CIL X,6093 (Caieta) **108**, 94
ILS 1660 = CIL VI,8517 (Rome) **115**, 99
ILS 1836 = CIL VI,8972 (Rome) **69**, 62
ILS 1914 = CIL III,6759 (Ankara) **116**, 100
ILS 1949 = CIL XIV,2298 (Rome) **42**, 40
ILS 1984 = CIL XIV,1437 (Ostia) **45**, 43
ILS 3018 = CIL V,4241 (Concesi, Italy) **40**, 40
ILS 3025 = CIL III,6456 (Aquincum/Budapest) **27**, 32
ILS 3521 = CIL VI,623 (Rome) **165**, 144
ILS 3598 = CIL VII,237 (York) **29**, 33
ILS 3604 = CIL II,1980 (Adra, Spain) **31**, 33
ILS 3608 = CIL IX,725 (Morrone, France) **32**, 34
ILS 3643 = CIL VI,259 (Rome) **30**, 33
ILS 3644 = CIL VIII,3695 (Lambaesis, North Africa) **28**, 32
ILS 3751 = CIL VIII,18890 (Thibilis, Numidia) **159**, 139
ILS 3840 = CIL VI,30983 (Rome) **97**, 83
ILS 4034 = CIL XI,7485 (Falerii) **41**, 40
ILS 4514b = CIL II,2403 (Caldas de Vizella,
   Portugal) **137**, 116
ILS 4682 = CIL XIII,2873 (Alesia) **160**, 140
ILS 4999 = CIL VI,2210 (Rome) **107**, 94
ILS 5010 = CIL VI,2170 (Rome) **194**, 163
ILS 6093 = CIL I,532 (Fundi) **212**, 179
ILS 6106 = CIL VI,1492 (Rome) **213**, 180
ILS 7217 = CIL XI,2702 (Volsinii) **211**, 179
ILS 8379a = CIL VI,10229 (Rome) **158**, 134
ILS 8393 = CIL VI,1527 (Rome) **52**, 49
ILS 8394 = CIL VI,10230 (Rome) **157**, 132
ILS 8402 = CIL VI,11602 (Rome) **53**, 52
ILS 8403 = CIL I,1007 (Rome) **54**, 52
ILS 8417 = CIL I,1479 (Cartagena, Spain) **76**, 65
ILS 8422 = CIL VI,7595 (Rome) **77**, 65
ILS 8430 = CIL VI,20158 and 20116 (Rome) **51**, 47
ILS 8432 = CIL VI,22355a (Rome) **46**, 43
ILS 8436 = CIL VI,8012 (Rome) **73**, 64
ILS 8437 = CIL IX,1913 (Benevento) **57**, 54

# SELECT BIBLIOGRAPHY

## Roman society

J. Carcopino, *Daily Life in Ancient Rome* (English translation first published London, 1940, many reprints).

J. A. Crook, *Law and Life of Rome* (London, 1967).

A. O. W. Dilke, *The Ancient Romans: How they Lived and Worked* (Newton Abbot, 1975).

L. Friedländer, *Roman Life and Manners under the Early Empire* (4 vols, 1908–13; = *Darstellungen aus der Sittengeschichte Roms*, Leipzig, 1919–22).

P. D. A. Garnsey and R. P. Saller, *The Roman Empire: Economy, Society and Culture* (London, 1987).

J. Hallett, *Fathers and Daughters* (Princeton, 1984).

K. Hopkins, *Conquerors and Slaves* (Cambridge, 1978).

K. Hopkins, *Death and Renewal* (Cambridge, 1983).

R. MacMullen, *Roman Social Relations 50 BC–AD 284* (New Haven, 1974).

B. Rawson (ed.), *The Family in Ancient Rome* (London, 1986).

H. Strasburger, *Zum Antiken Gesellschaftsideal* (Heidelberg, 1976).

P. H. J. Thomas, *Introduction to Roman Law* (Deventer, 1986), chs 5 and 6.

P. Veyne (ed.), *A History of Private Life, I: from Pagan Rome to Byzantium* (translated by A. Goldhammer, Cambridge, Mass. and London, 1987).

## Composition and definition

K. R. Bradley, 'Dislocation in the Roman Family', *Historical Reflections/ Reflexions Historiques* 14, no. 1 (1987), 33–62.

K. R. Bradley, 'Remarriage and the Structure of the Upper-Class Roman Family', paper to the Second Canberra Conference on the Roman Family, July 1988.

R. Saller, '*Familia, Domus*, and the Roman Conception of the Family', *Phoenix* 38 (1984), 336–55.

B. D. Shaw, 'Latin Funerary Epigraphy and Family Life in the Later Roman Empire', *Historia* 33 (1984), 457–97.

# SELECT BIBLIOGRAPHY

B. D. Shaw, 'The Family in Late Antiquity: the Experience of Augustine', *Past and Present* no. 115 (1987), 3–51.

## Patria Potestas

J. A. Crook, *'Patria Potestas'*, *Classical Quarterly* 17 (1967), 113–22.

W. V. Harris, 'The Roman Father's Power of Life and Death', in R. S. Bagnell and W. V. Harris (eds), *Studies in Roman Law in Memory of A. Arthur Schiller* (Leiden, 1986), 81–95.

W. K. Lacey, *'Patria potestas'*, in Beryl Rawson (ed.), *The Family in Ancient Rome* (London, 1986), 121–44.

R. P. Saller, *'Patria potestas* and the Stereotype of the Roman Family', *Continuity and Change* 1 (1986), 7–22.

A. Watson, *Society and Legal Change* (Edinburgh, 1977), ch. 3.

## Houses

A. G. McKay, *Houses, Villas and Palaces in the Roman World* (Ithaca, 1976).

J. Percival, *The Roman Villa* (London, 1976).

Y. Thébert, 'Private Life and Domestic Architecture in Roman Africa', in P. Veyne (ed.), *A History of Private Life I: from Pagan Rome to Byzantium* (translated A. Goldhammer, Cambridge, Mass. and London, 1987), 313–409.

A. F. Wallace-Hadrill, 'The Social Structure of the Roman House', *Papers of the British School at Rome* 56 (1988), 43–97.

## Religion

A. Dubourdieu, *Les origines et le développement du culte des Pénates à Rome* (Rome, Ecole Française, 1989).

D. P. Harman, 'The Family Festivals of Rome', *Aufstieg und Niedergang der römischen Welt* II,16.2 (Berlin and New York, 1978), 1592–603.

D. G. Orr, 'Roman Domestic Religion – The Evidence of Household Shrines', *Aufstieg und Niedergang der römischen Welt* II,16.2 (Berlin and New York, 1978), 1557–91.

## Women

J. P. V. D. Balsdon, *Roman Women* (London, 1962).

A. Cameron and A. Kuhrt (eds), *Images of Women in Antiquity* (London, 1983).

G. Clark, 'Roman Women', *Greece & Rome* 28 (1981), 193–212.

S. Dixon, *The Roman Mother* (London, 1988).

J. Gardner, *Women in Roman Law and Society* (London, 1986).

N. Kampen, *Image and Status: Roman Working Women in Ostia* (Berlin, 1981).

M. R. Lefkowitz and M. B. Fant, *Women's Life in Greece and Rome* (London, 1982).

S. B. Pomeroy, *Goddesses, Whores, Wives, and Slaves: Women in Classical Antiquity* (New York, 1975).

## Tutela

F. Schulz, *Classical Roman Law* (Oxford, 1951), ch. 5.

A. Watson, *The Law of Persons at Rome* (Oxford, 1967), chs 9–12.

## Marital relations and ideals

P. Brown, 'Late Antiquity' in P. Veyne (ed.), *A History of Private Life I: from Pagan Rome to Byzantium* (translated A. Goldhammer, Cambridge, Mass. and London, 1987), 235–311.

P. E. Corbett, *The Roman Law of Marriage* (Oxford, 1930).

P. Csillag, *The Augustan Laws on Family Relations* (Budapest, 1976).

M. Durry, *Eloge Funèbre d'une Matrone Romaine* (Paris, 1950).

H. L. Gordon, 'The Eternal Triangle, First Century BC', *Classical Journal* 28 (1932–3), 574–8.

J. Griffin, 'Augustan Poetry and the Life of Luxury', JRS 66 (1976), 87–105.

M. K. Hopkins, 'The Age of Roman Girls at Marriage', *Population Studies* 18 (1965), 309–27.

G. Huzar, 'Mark Antony's Wives', *Classical Journal* 81 (1986), 97–111.

R. Lattimore, *Themes in Greek and Latin Epitaphs* (Urbana, 1942).

N. Purcell, 'Livia and the Womanhood of Rome', *Proceedings of the Cambridge Philological Society* 32 (1986), 78–105.

B. Rawson, 'Roman Concubinage', *Transactions of the American Philological Association* 104 (1974), 279ff.

B. D. Shaw, 'The Age of Roman Girls at Marriage: some Reconsiderations', JRS 77 (1987), 30–46.

G. Williams, 'Some Aspects of Roman Marriage Ceremonies and Ideals', JRS 48 (1958), 16–29.

E. Wistrand, *The So-Called Laudatio Turiae* (Lund, 1976).

## Children and upbringing

A. D. Booth, 'The Schooling of Slaves in First-century AD Rome', *Transactions of the American Philological Association* 109 (1979), 11ff.

K. R. Bradley, 'Child Care at Rome: The Role of Men', *Historical Reflections/Reflexions Historiques* 12 (1985), 485–523.

C. A. Forbes, 'The Education and Training of Slaves', *Transactions of the American Philological Association* 86 (1955), 321–60.

M. L. Gordon, 'The Freedman's Son in Municipal Life', JRS 21 (1931), 65ff.

H. I. Marrou, *History of Education in Antiquity* (1948; many edns, English translation 1956).

J. P. Neraudau, *Etre Enfant à Rome* (Paris, 1984).

H. S. Nielsen, '*Alumnus*: a Term of Relation denoting Quasi-Adoption', *Classica et Medievalia* 38 (1987), 141–88.

# SELECT BIBLIOGRAPHY

T. E. J. Wiedemann, *Adults and Children in the Roman Empire* (London, 1989).

## Slavery

K. Bradley, *Slaves and Masters in the Roman Empire* (Brussels, 1984; Oxford, 1987).

P. A. Brunt, 'Evidence given under Torture in the Principate', *Zeitschrift der Savigny-Stiftung für Rechtsgeschichte. Romanistische Abteilung* 97 (1980), 256–65.

W. V. Harris, 'Towards a Study of the Roman Slave Trade', *Memoirs of the American Academy at Rome* 36 (1980), 117–40.

O. Patterson, *Slavery and Social Death* (Cambridge, Mass., 1982).

W. D. Philips, Jr, *Slavery from Roman Times to the Early Transatlantic Trade* (Minnesota and Manchester, 1985).

S. Treggiari, 'Family Life among the Staff of the Volusii', *Transactions of the American Philological Association* 105 (1975), 393–401.

S. Treggiari, 'Jobs in the Household of Livia', *Papers of the British School at Rome* 43 (1975), 48–77.

A. Watson, *Roman Slave Law* (Baltimore and London, 1987).

T. E. J. Wiedemann, *Slavery* (New Surveys in the Classics no.19: Oxford, 1987).

## Property

E. Champlin, 'Owners and Neighbours at Ligures Baebiani', *Chiron* 11 (1981), 239–64.

M. I. Finley (ed.), *Studies in Roman Property* (Cambridge, 1976), esp. chs 5 and 7.

B. W. Frier, 'Cicero's Management of his Urban Properties', *Classical Journal* 74 (1978), 1–6.

B. W. Frier, 'The Rental Market in Early Imperial Rome', JRS 67 (1977), 27–37.

B. W. Frier, *Landlords and Tenants in Imperial Rome* (Princeton, 1980).

P. D. Garnsey, 'Urban Property Investment', in M. I. Finley (ed.), *Studies in Roman Property* (Cambridge, 1976), 123ff.

## The economics of the household

J. Andreau, *Les Affaires de Monsieur Jucundus* (Rome, 1974).

J. H. D'Arms, *Commerce and Social Standing in Ancient Rome* (Harvard, 1981).

R. Duncan-Jones, *The Economy of the Roman Empire* (Cambridge, 1982), esp. chs. 1 and 2.

M. I. Finley, *The Ancient Economy* (London, 1973).

J. M. Frayn, *Subsistence Farming in Roman Italy* (London, 1979).

J. M. Frayn, *Sheep-rearing and the Wool Trade in Italy during the Roman Period* (Liverpool, 1984).

P. Garnsey (ed.), *Non-Slave Labour in the Greco-Roman World* (Cambridge, 1980).

P. D. A. Garnsey, K. Hopkins and C. R. Whittaker (eds), *Trade in the Ancient Economy* (London, 1983).

# THE ROMAN HOUSEHOLD

P. D. A. Garnsey and C. R. Whittaker (eds), *Trade and Famine in Classical Antiquity* (Cambridge, 1983).

D. P. Kehoe, *The Economics of Agriculture on Roman Imperial Estates in North Africa*, Hypomnemata 89 (Göttingen, 1988).

D. Manacorda, 'The Ager Cosanus and the Production of the Amphorae of Sestius', JRS 68 (1978), 122–31.

T. W. Potter, *The Changing Landscape of South Etruria* (London, 1979).

N. Purcell, 'Wine and Wealth in Ancient Italy', JRS 75 (1985), 1–19.

D. W. Rathbone, 'The Development of Agriculture in the Ager Cosanus during the Roman Republic: Problems of Evidence and Interpretation' (review article), JRS 71 (1981), 10–23.

D. W. Rathbone, 'The Slave Mode of Production in Italy' (review article), JRS 73 (1983), 160–8.

I. Shatzman, *Senatorial Wealth and Roman Politics* (Brussels, 1975).

K. D. White, *Roman Farming* (London, 1970).

K. D. White, *Country Life in Classical Times* (London, 1977).

For slaves and day-labourers in Roman Palestine, cf. references in the *Mishnah*, translated H. Danby (Oxford, 1933); M. Goodman, *State and Society in Roman Galilee* (Totowa, NJ, 1983).

## The old

S. Bertman (ed.), *The Conflict of Generations in Ancient Greece and Rome* (Amsterdam, 1976).

E. Eyben, 'Old Age in Greco-Roman Antiquity and Early Christianity: An Annotated Select Bibliography', in: T. A. Falkner and J. de Luce (eds), *Old Age in Greek and Latin Literature* (Albany, NY, 1989), 230–51.

C. Gnilka, 'Altersversorgung', *Realencyclopaedie für Antike und Christentum* suppl. vol. 1–2 (1985), col. 266–89.

## Life-expectancy

P. A. Brunt, *Italian Manpower* (Oxford, 1971), ch. XI (pp. 131ff.), XXI (385ff.).

R. P. Duncan-Jones, 'Age-rounding, Illiteracy and Social Differentiation in the Roman Empire', *Chiron* 7 (1977), 333–53.

R. P. Duncan-Jones, 'Age-rounding in Greco-Roman Egypt', ZPE 33 (1979), 169–77.

B. Frier, 'Roman Life Expectancy: Ulpian's Evidence', *Harvard Studies in Classical Philology* 86 (1982), 213–51.

B. Frier, 'Roman Life Expectancy: The Pannonian Evidence', *Phoenix* 37 (1983), 328–44.

K. Hopkins, 'On the Probable Age-Structure of the Roman Population', *Population Studies* 20 (1966), 245–64.

R. P. Saller, 'Men's Age at Marriage and its Consequences in the Roman Family', *Classical Philology* 82 (1987), 21–34.

# SELECT BIBLIOGRAPHY

R. P. Saller and B. D. Shaw, 'Tombstones and Roman Family Relations in the Principate: Civilians, Soldiers and Slaves', JRS, 74 (1984), 124–56.

## Infanticide, abortion and birth control

E. Boswell, 'Exposition and *Oblatio*: The Abandonment of Children and the Ancient and Medieval Family', *American Historical Review* 89 (1984), 10–33.

D. Engels, 'The Problem of Female Infanticide in the Greco-Roman World', *Classical Philology* 75 (1980), 112–20.

E. Eyben, 'Family Planning in Greco-Roman Antiquity', *Ancient Society* 11–12 (1980–1), 5–82.

P. Garnsey, 'Trajan's *Alimenta*', *Historia* 17 (1968), 367–81.

M. Golden, 'Demography and the Exposure of Girls at Athens', *Phoenix* 35 (1981), 316–31.

W. V. Harris, 'The Theoretical Possibility of Extensive Infanticide in the Greco-Roman World', *Classical Quarterly* 32 (1982), 114–16.

W. J. Watts, 'Ovid, the Law and Roman Society on Abortion', *Acta Classica* 16 (1973), 89–101.

## Inheritance

E. Champlin, '*Creditur vulgo testamenta hominum speculum esse morum*: Why the Romans made Wills', *Classical Philology* 84 (1989), 198–215.

J. Crook, *Law and Life of Rome* (London, 1967).

R. P. Saller, 'Roman Dowry and the Devolution of Property in the Principate', *Classical Quarterly* 34 (1984), 195–205.

R. Syme, 'The *Testamentum Dasumii*. Some Novelties', *Chiron* 15 (1985), 41–63 = *Roman Papers* V (Oxford, 1988), 521–43.

A. Wallace-Hadrill, 'Family and Inheritance in the Augustan Marriage Laws', *Proceedings of the Cambridge Philological Society* 27 (1981), 58–80.

## The *Testamentum Porcelli*

B. Baldwin, 'The *Testamentum Porcelli*', in *Studies in Late Roman and Byzantine History, Literature and Language* (Amsterdam, 1984), 137–48.

E. Champlin, 'The Testament of the Piglet', *Phoenix* 41 (1987), 174–83.

D. Daube, *Roman Law. Linguistic, Social and Philosophical Aspects* (Edinburgh, 1967), 78–91.

## Manumission and freedmen

A. M. Duff, *Freedmen in the Early Roman Empire* (Oxford, 1928).

S. Treggiari, *Roman Freedmen during the Late Republic* (Oxford, 1969).

W. Waldstein, *Operae Libertorum* (Stuttgart, 1986), reviewed in *Classical Review* 38, no. 2 (1988), 331–3.

# THE ROMAN HOUSEHOLD

T. E. J. Wiedemann, 'The Regularity of Manumission at Rome', *Classical Quarterly* 35 (1985), 162–75.

## Patronage and friendship

J. Crook, *Consilium Principis* (Cambridge, 1955).

E. Gellner and J. Waterbury (eds), *Patrons and Clients in Mediterranean Societies* (London, 1977).

G. Herman, *Ritualised Friendship and the Greek City* (Cambridge, 1986).

J. M. Kelly, *Roman Litigation* (Oxford, 1971), ch. 2.

R. P. Saller, *Personal Patronage under the Early Empire* (Cambridge, 1982).

A. Wallace-Hadrill (ed.), *Patronage in Ancient Society* (London, 1989).

## Some comparisons

E. M. Craik (ed.), *Marriage and Property* (Aberdeen, 1984).

J. Goody, 'Slavery in Time and Space', J. L. Watson (ed.), *Asian and African Systems of Slavery* (Oxford, 1980), 16–42.

J. Goody, J. Thirsk and E. P. Thompson (eds), *Family and Inheritance: Rural Society in Western Europe 1200–1800* (Cambridge, 1976).

R. A. Houlbrooke, *The English Family, 1450–1700* (London, 1984).

P. Laslett and R. Wall (eds), *Household and Family in Past Time* (Cambridge, 1972).

A. Macfarlane, *Marriage and Love in England 1300–1840* (Oxford, 1986).

J. G. Peristiany, *Mediterranean Family Structures* (Cambridge, 1976).

# INDEX

This index includes references to passages from ancient sources mentioned in the text, but not those excerpts already listed in the Index of Passages Cited. Where persons had several names, they are listed by the one by which they are usually designated (e.g., M. Tullius Cicero under 'C').

# INDEX